USES OF DATE OF BIRTH

USES OF DATE OF BIRTH

OLATUNJI OLUSANYA

USES OF DATE OF BIRTH
By Olatunji Olusanya

Copyright © 2025 by Olatunji Olusanya

Published by Baruch Publishing - 07908684207
Contact Copyright Holder at
Olatunji Olusanya
Email: tunjato45@yahoo.com
Tel: 07403 232433

All rights are reserved. No part of this publication may be reproduced, stored in a retrieval system or transmitted in any form or by any means, electronic, mechanical, photocopying, recording or otherwise, without prior permission of Olatunji Olusanya

Cover & Interior Design by Karl Hunt

ISBN 979-8-89686-414-1

CONTENTS

Preface vii
Introduction ix

CHAPTER 1: When a Child Is Born 1

CHAPTER 2: How Did You Come to the Word? 6

CHAPTER 3: Child Delivery 10

CHAPTER 4: Naming Ceremony 15

CHAPTER 5: Repeating One's Name 19

CHAPTER 6: Invention of Information Technology 23

CHAPTER 7: Your Family Tree 29

CHAPTER 8: Argument about Age Seniority 34

CHAPTER 9: At Every Reception 39

CHAPTER 10: Online Uses of Date of Birth 42

CHAPTER 11: Plants and Flowers Are Planted in Dates 49

CHAPTER 12: Time Is Money   54

CHAPTER 13: Changing the Clock's Time   59

CHAPTER 14: Memorable Dates   64

CHAPTER 15: The Race for Time   70

CHAPTER 16: The African Virtues   75

CHAPTER 17: Time Flies   82

CHAPTER 18: The World of Tomorrow   86

CHAPTER 19: Living with Artificial Intelligence and Robot   90

CHAPTER 20: Travelling in the Modern World   95

CHAPTER 21: When Retired from Work   103

CHAPTER 22: The Future as It Should Be   109

CHAPTER 23: The Concept of African Times   114

CHAPTER 24: Life Could Be Made Better   118

About the Author   124

PREFACE

The inspiration for this book stems from a singular yet universal detail: Date of Birth. This fundamental aspect of life, often recorded and quickly forgotten, wields an outsized influence over our identities, opportunities, and perceptions of self. From childhood to old age, our Date of Birth becomes a constant reference point, dictating the timing of rights, responsibilities, and societal expectations.

Throughout this work, I aim to unpack the layered significance of the Date of Birth, particularly in the contexts of Nigeria and the UK. These two societies, though distinct in history and culture, both reveal intriguing parallels in how this single fact governs individual and systemic outcomes.

This book seeks not only to provoke thought but also to challenge conventional narratives. It explores how this fundamental marker intersects with power, privilege, and marginalisation, and questions the fairness of its sometimes arbitrary influence on lives.

I hope that readers, through the chapters ahead, will gain a new appreciation for the hidden complexities behind such a seemingly simple part of our identity. May it inspire deeper reflection on how systems of governance and cultural norms can adapt to ensure fairness and inclusivity for all.

Warm regards,

Olatunji Olusanya

INTRODUCTION

The humble *Date of Birth*–a collection of numbers seemingly innocuous on the surface–possesses an undeniable power that has woven itself into the fabric of our personal identities and societal systems. From the moment we enter the world, this singular timestamp begins to influence how we are perceived, treated, and categorised within various cultural, legal, and administrative frameworks. But have we ever paused to reflect on the multifaceted role this date plays beyond its utility in marking anniversaries or celebrations of life?

Throughout history, the uses of *Date of Birth* have evolved from a mere reference point for age to a tool wielded with significant consequences. Governments use it to enforce regulations, institutions rely on it for record-keeping, and employers use it to assess eligibility and suitability. Even the realms of health and education adapt their frameworks based on our arrival date, subtly dictating opportunities and pathways that shape our lives. And yet, beneath its seeming objectivity lies a complex interaction with societal biases, historical contexts, and human behaviour that often goes unnoticed.

In this exploration of the *Date of Birth*, I delve into its layered significance, examining how it governs systems, influences relationships, and, at times, serves as a point of contention in determining access and privilege. What does this unassuming detail reveal about us as individuals and the societies we inhabit? How have its applications affected notions of equity, opportunity, and identity across generations?

This narrative unravels these questions, casting light on a mundane yet pivotal piece of information that defines who we are, how we engage with the world, and the stories we tell ourselves about time and existence.

CHAPTER ONE
WHEN A CHILD IS BORN

Every living soul has both a date of birth and death. As we often remarked in those years when we shared jokes in gatherings of elders reflecting on life, just as everyone celebrates a day of birth, there is also a destined day when each person reaches their final destination in the journey of life.

The date of birth holds great significance in a person's life. Regardless of where one is born–whether at home, as was customary in Africa during the 1940s and 1950s with the assistance of a native herbalist acting as a midwife under the rudimentary methods of childbirth, or in an ambulance, perhaps even in a car while en route to the hospital, or with the timely aid of a medical doctor at the hospital–the act of recording the event is crucial. Except in those early primitive times, the person attending the delivery would typically note the time, date, and ensure an accurate record of the birth.

A naming ceremony in Africa is often conducted as a religious ritual to mark the occasion on the eighth day after a child's birth. On the ninth day, one of the parents or a relative–typically the father, an uncle or aunt–may proceed to the registry office to officially record the child's birth. However, in unfortunate circumstances, such as a premature birth or when a child fails to cry at birth, the situation brings immense sorrow to the couple. These occurrences, though rare, are deeply distressing and not events anyone prays to experience.

Every child is born to a woman, either through a sexual relationship with a man or via In Vitro Fertilisation (IVF). IVF is a medical procedure by which a woman becomes pregnant through the surgical introduction of sperm from a man into her womb. Couples unable to conceive naturally often opt for this method to fulfil their desire to become parents. In such cases, the man is still regarded as the legal and biological father of the child.

Another form of IVF involves the use of a surrogate. Here, the sperm from a man is injected into the womb of a woman who is not his wife, under a contractual agreement. The arrangement typically includes financial provisions for the surrogate during her pregnancy, as well as compensation after she delivers the child and hands it over to the biological father and his partner.

Modern civilisation and the application of technology have transformed the date of birth into a new gateway through which an individual's identity can be easily and authentically traced, whether formally authorised or without the person's consent. Regardless of the context, once your date of birth is known, you effectively become public property.

In today's world, whether seeking employment, joining a social club, contacting a general practice (GP) reception to book an appointment, or collecting medication from a pharmacy, your name has lost its prominence as the primary means of identification. Instead, your date of birth takes precedence. Even the customary enquiry, 'To whom am I speaking, please?' has become a mere formality, as the only information of real utility to many organisations is your date of birth.

For instance, imagine being taken to a police station on suspicion of a minor offence, perhaps reported by a bystander, merely because you were found in the vicinity of the incident. The attending officers are required to interrogate you to determine your connection, if any, to the alleged crime. As part of the process, the police typically take your particulars–name, date of birth, residential address, and possibly your place of work–to facilitate further investigations. In some cases, they might confiscate your passport to ensure you do not leave the country while investigations are ongoing.

Initially, you might attempt to provide a false name or address. However, during interrogation at the station, your date of birth will reveal your true identity. Any claims that the officers misheard your name will no longer hold weight, as your date of birth will uncover any past criminal records when entered into the system.

This reliance on the date of birth as a primary identifier poses unique challenges for black individuals in the United Kingdom and across many European countries. A common claim in these contexts is that police officers misunderstood or misrecorded names due to pronunciation or dialect. Nevertheless, such misunderstandings are ultimately rendered irrelevant, as the date of birth remains the definitive key to tracing one's identity and records.

Let us assume you wish to verify a piece of information from the Home Office regarding your application for a grant of permanent residency in the country, which your solicitor has submitted on your behalf. While asking for your name might appear to be a matter of politeness or friendliness, the crucial detail they would rely upon to trace your records is your date of birth. This is because many individuals could share the same surname, and possibly even the same first name, but it is exceedingly rare for two people to share both names and the same date of birth.

For instance, when an individual is apprehended on public transport in London for failing to pay the full fare for the length of their journey, inspectors will request documentary evidence bearing their name. Simply providing one's name verbally may not be sufficiently convincing to establish identity. Inspectors would typically ask for the person's date of birth to ensure they are dealing with a verified individual, not an artificial intelligence (AI) masquerading as human. In contemporary official interactions, merely stating your name is no longer considered authentic, trustworthy, or acceptable as definitive proof of identity.

It is not uncommon for two or more individuals to incidentally share the same first and last names; however, they are unlikely to share the same date of birth. I have personally encountered two individuals from different families who shared identical first and last names and were born in the same month and year, yet their exact dates of birth were distinctly different.

In some instances, individuals may seek to alter or amend their dates of birth. This process can be protracted and requires considerable justification, as the person must persuade the relevant authorities handling such requests. The reasons for seeking such a change must be compelling, and the individual's age is often scrutinised with the questions that arise during the verification process. Additionally, they may need to account for their actions since becoming aware of the discrepancy in their recorded date of birth.

Records must be carefully searched and scrutinised to ensure that individuals requesting a change of date of birth are not attempting to conceal past criminal activities. In Nigeria, where corruption, favouritism, bribery, and dishonesty thrive and have become entrenched in daily life, negligence in handling cases is common. Crimes are often abandoned without substantive grounds, leaving no precedent or evidence for future cases to reference. This lack of precedential rulings or judgements from Superior Courts creates a gap, depriving future cases of a guiding framework for similar circumstances. As life evolves, human behaviours and the environment continue to change. Therefore, we must recognise that nothing in this universe remains static.

CHAPTER TWO

HOW DID YOU COME TO THE WORD?

According to [1]Worldometer (2024), the world population is reported to have exceeded eight billion people. Based on the United Nations member states, over 195 countries are inhabiting the Earth. Each of these nations strives to be recognised as distinct from one another through their unique cultures, traditions, languages, cuisines, and traditional attire. Alongside these distinctions, the Creator fashioned humanity with diverse characteristics, such as facial features, height, language, dietary habits, and eating customs. Our skin, often referred to as complexion, is influenced by the geographical environments in which we live and serves as a visible determinant of our external appearance–often linked to the concept of race.

People come into the world through various modes of conception. Some couples (men and women) maintain relationships for several years before deciding to formalise their union through marriage. Subsequently, the woman may become pregnant

---

1   Use this link https://shorturl.at/RatnD to confirm the world population

and give birth to a healthy baby, irrespective of its sex (male or female). In other cases, some individuals meet and, after a few social interactions or visits, the woman becomes pregnant and later gives birth to a child. There are also instances where women become pregnant during relationships with boyfriends who, for various reasons, may deny responsibility for the pregnancy. If the woman is financially independent, whether through employment, trade, or business, she may choose to keep the pregnancy and eventually give birth to a child. Such women are often referred to as 'single mothers'.

On the one hand, some women engage in social outings with men willing to pay the price they demand. Despite taking medical precautions to avoid situations that could hinder their source of income, they are often surprised to find themselves pregnant without a specific man to identify as the father when the child is born. On the other hand, some legally married couples face difficulties in bearing children due to medical issues affecting either the man or the woman. Desperate to have a child they can call their own, they may explore two available options.

The first option is *in vitro fertilisation* (IVF), a widely known medical procedure. Through IVF, the man's sperm is collected in a medical laboratory or IVF clinic and scientifically injected into the woman's womb. However, no empirical research confirms that this procedure automatically results in pregnancy. The process may fail on the first or even the second attempt, and successful results are not guaranteed immediately.

The second option involves surrogacy. This approach entails extracting sperm from the husband and injecting it into another woman, different from his wife, who agrees to carry the baby.

In such cases, the wife, often aware of her medical limitations, consents to this arrangement in consultation with her husband. Surrogacy has also gained popularity among some male celebrities in partnerships with other men, enabling them to have children.

The legal framework surrounding surrogacy ensures that once all contractual terms are fulfilled, the surrogate mother is compensated as agreed and relinquishes all claims to the child. She is legally prohibited from asserting any maternal rights or publicly claiming to be the mother of the child under any circumstances.

Turning to another societal issue, an alarming number of rape cases are reported daily in Nigerian national and local newspapers. These cases, often under police investigation, highlight a pervasive problem. Rape is defined as a situation where a man has sexual intercourse with a woman without her consent. However, such allegations can occasionally be used by women to disgrace or implicate men due to personal vendettas. That said, engaging in non-consensual sex is a criminal offence. If proven beyond a reasonable doubt in a court of law with substantial evidence, the perpetrator may face a prison sentence of up to ten years without the option of a fine.

Teachers have been reported in the newspapers to have forcefully had sexual intercourse with underaged school children put in their care. Adult men both married and single are often reported to have raped their house-girls or housemaids. Many married men have been reported to rape their wife's younger sisters given by the family to the couple so they could look after the wife's welfare. Some men were detained and put in Police custody for raping mentally ill ladies that are living and sleeping under the bridge. If any of these incidents results in a pregnancy, a child will be born regardless of the condition of birth, and may end up being irrelevant.

Different laws operate in different countries on the issue of illegally born children, some countries made law that every child must be catered for by the state whether the child is legitimate or illegitimate. These apply to a situation where a woman may give birth to a child secretly in their home toilet, wrap the child in old clothes, bags or towels and abandon it at a road junction so that it would be seen and taken to the hospital for thorough examinations and probably be given a name. Its date of birth may be accurately determined through medical tests and examinations or the day the child was discovered may be adopted as the date it was born. The name of the person who first sighted and made report on the child and probably called the police or the ambulance that subsequently take it to the hospital may be recorded as the name of the child depending on its gender.

That confirms the saying that we are not born equally.

CHAPTER THREE
CHILD DELIVERY

Blessed are the nations that spread the knowledge and bravery of their citizens by sharing their experiences and adventurous journeys of experimentation with other countries, allowing the gifts of God within them to be felt and enjoyed across borders. The ventures of the early explorers could be regarded as the riskiest undertakings imaginable. Deciding to journey to a place where no one has ever been and then return to recount the existing conditions, the environment, and the inhabitants encountered, greatly aids the preparations of future expeditions. It enables subsequent voyagers to anticipate what to expect, prepare adequately, and form a mental image of the journey ahead–thereby diminishing fear. Such an endeavour is far from an easy task.

Africa was once perceived as an enigmatic and impenetrable sphere by European inhabitants, earning it the moniker *the Dark Continent.* This term did not solely reference the external atmosphere or the skin colour of its people but rather the perceived mysteries and challenges of the land itself. Historical accounts reveal that some early explorers never returned to share their findings. Many rivers upon which they navigated turned out to be treacherous waterfalls, leading to sudden capsizes and instant deaths. Additionally, records suggest that some African tribes of the time killed and consumed these explorers. While such claims cannot be entirely verified, neither can they be wholly dismissed.

Each of us has a history tied to our birth, but I do not subscribe to the notion that people are born with mysterious inscriptions on their left hands, as some propagators of myth might claim. Our historical experiences and life narratives are shaped by the events after birth. Life after death is, in my view, a mirage–a concept used to instil fear and panic, distracting people from pursuing inspirational and adventurous endeavours that could immortalise their names. Fear cripples ambition, doubt undermines determination, and weakness derails focus. Unless one overcomes these impediments, little can be achieved in the pursuit of creating a lasting legacy.

In Africa, our forefathers served as nurses and doctors to our mothers through the use of herbal remedies, a practice inherited from past generations. When a woman was due to give birth, the herbalist in charge would ask everyone, including the woman's husband, to leave the vicinity. Before doing so, the herbalist would ensure that a fire was already burning, prepared in advance of his arrival. The pregnant woman would then be asked to remove all clothing, standing naked with her back facing the fire.

This positioning, rather than directly facing the fire, seemed rooted in the local understanding of scientific principles at the time. It was believed that the heat from the fire would cause discomfort to the baby within the womb, prompting it to seek escape and resulting in a safe delivery.

This book does not aim to weigh the benefits and risks of such traditional methods in Africa, nor to compare them with the European medical system practised in modern hospitals. It suffices to say that these traditional methods often worked but came with side effects, which, in the absence of formal education, were sometimes attributed to the work of devils, enemies, or Satan. While there were instances where mothers or babies experienced post-birth health issues, it is important to acknowledge that European medical practices also come with challenges, both pre- and post-delivery. As Christians and Muslims alike profess in their faiths, every birth occurs as designed by the Lord or Allah, and no method is entirely free of human error or complications.

There are accounts of mothers giving birth in unexpected circumstances, highlighting the unpredictability of childbirth. Some women have delivered their babies in cars while being driven to the hospital, with their husbands offering support learned through online resources or medical training.

One noteworthy account involved a working-class woman who went to work as usual, despite being pregnant, as her due date, according to the doctor, was still some weeks away. During the staff lunch break, her waters unexpectedly broke, and she began crying out for help. Her female colleagues quickly gathered around her in a circle to preserve her privacy. While some called for medical assistance, others with knowledge of childbirth stepped in to help. By the time the medical team arrived, she had successfully delivered a healthy baby girl. The remainder of the process was simply a formality, as mother and child were taken to the hospital for examinations and reassurance that all was well.

Whenever a child is born, the first cardinal rule is to record the exact time of delivery. This includes noting the time in seconds, minutes, and hours, as well as the date, month, and year.

These details are essential as they will be officially recorded on the birth certificate at the registrar's office.

In Europe, couples often decide on a name for their child once a doctor confirms the pregnancy and informs them of the baby's gender during prenatal consultations. Medical tests, such as ultrasounds, can help the medical team determine the gender of the child while it is still in the womb. This allows parents to select a name in advance. In cases where a miscarriage sadly occurs, some couples still document the incident, using the name they had chosen for the child, even though it was a foetus at the time.

On the other hand, in Africa, it has not traditionally been part of our culture to name a child before seeing or holding them in our arms. Additionally, until recently, our medical facilities were not developed enough to determine the gender of a child in the womb. While this test may now be available in a few private hospitals, it often comes at a cost far beyond the reach of ordinary citizens. In government hospitals, the facilities required for such tests remain largely unavailable, making it challenging to confirm a baby's gender before birth.

In general, the naming of a newborn in Africa occurs on the eighth day after birth. Parents usually invite their religious leaders–whether Christian, Muslim, or traditionalist–to officiate the naming ceremony. Among the Yoruba, for instance, traditionalists of the Ìṣèṣe faith, which represents the inherited religion of Yoruba origin, are often invited to give the child a name that the family intends them to bear for life. Due to these customary practices, a birth certificate is typically not issued until the child has been formally named.

Reports have emerged of schoolgirls who became pregnant

while living under their parents' roofs. Remarkably, they managed to conceal their pregnancies from their parents despite residing in the same household. In some instances, these girls gave birth in the toilet, at which point the secret could no longer be kept. Their parents often found themselves acting as emergency midwives during the delivery.

In other cases, births occurred in hostels or rented accommodations, unknown to those they lived with. To avoid the stigma of being discovered or the responsibility of raising a child, some girls wrapped the newborn in towels or old clothes that could not be traced through DNA. They would then abandon the baby in refuse bins far from their homes.

There are also reports of newborns left at road junctions or roundabouts overnight. In such cases, it is often early risers on their way to work who hear the baby's cries and alert the police. The authorities usually take the child to a hospital for thorough medical examinations to determine their health status and, in some instances, assign the child a name.

Additionally, some women face medical complications that prevent them from delivering naturally, even with advanced facilities available in hospitals. In such circumstances, caesarean sections are often arranged to prevent overdue pregnancies, which can lead to complications for both mother and child.

Children born after an extended stay in the womb have sometimes been reported to suffer from conditions caused by water or blood entering the brain. This can result in severe impairments, such as difficulty moving, speaking, or walking. Many children seen in wheelchairs with profound disabilities may have experienced such complications due to prolonged gestation.

CHAPTER FOUR

NAMING CEREMONY

Anywhere in the world, the date a child is born holds immense significance for the parents. The joy of a successful delivery is profoundly magical and beyond description. During labour, a woman endures hours of intense pain but is ultimately overcome with tears of joy as she holds her newborn in her arms for the first time. She aspires to provide the best care for her child within the limits of her financial resources.

The father, on the other hand, announces the birth to friends and family members. In Europe, it is customary for the man to remain by his wife's side in the delivery ward during childbirth. However, many African men shy away from witnessing the process for reasons that I shall not elaborate upon in this book. Nonetheless, after the birth, fathers are typically overwhelmed with gratitude. It is uncommon not to see them express their appreciation to God through gestures such as jumping for joy or bowing so deeply that their foreheads touch the floor, symbolising appreciation for a safe delivery.

[2]The Lancet reported in 2021 that '23 million miscarriages occur every year.' Such a report is staggering. These issues could be significantly mitigated with the provision of free, efficient, and standard prenatal care delivered by medically trained personnel equipped with adequate resources. Ensuring proper care for pregnant women should be a fundamental commitment of any government, particularly in safeguarding the welfare of its poorer and lower-class citizens.

Regardless of one's religious beliefs–Christian, Muslim, or traditional faiths like *Ìṣèṣe*–it is customary to invite a spiritual leader from the family's faith to bestow a name upon the newborn. This act provides spiritual protection and guidance for the child.

In Yoruba culture, the father gives the spiritual leader the name by which the child will be officially known and called. Similarly, in Christian traditions, the father selects the name for the child to be spiritually consecrated. This naming ceremony differs from the 40-day dedication when the child is brought to church for the first time. In Islam, the Imam or *Alfa* typically names the child, often selecting a name that honours one of the Prophet Muhammad's (S.A.W) followers, under Islamic principles.

The extent of a naming ceremony depends on several factors, including the financial capacity of the parents and how popular and respected they are within the community. I have witnessed instances where friends, associates, and family members

---

2   Quenby, S., Gallos, I. D., Dhillon-Smith, R. K., Podesek, M., Stephenson, M. D., Fisher, J., . . . & Coomarasamy, A. (2021). Miscarriage matters: the epidemiological, physical, psychological, and economic costs of early pregnancy loss. *The Lancet*, *397*(10285), 1658-1667.

contribute financially to support the celebrant, particularly when they are aware of the individual's limited resources–especially if the parents have waited for years, relying on divine intervention, to have a child.

Some naming ceremonies are so elaborate that the celebrations extend beyond the conclusion of the religious service. Parents with sufficient financial capacity might hire an event centre and engage a live musician to entertain guests throughout the night. From that day onward, the perception of the parents within the community transforms significantly. People who once addressed them by their given names adjust their behaviour, now honouring them as the father or mother of their child.

In African culture and tradition, this shift in identity is deeply symbolic. Parents are often referred to as *Bàbá* (the father) or *Màmá* (the mother) followed by the child's name. Only those in their age group or older retain the courtesy and privilege of addressing them by their original names. It is believed that God has bestowed upon them a new name and a garment of honour. Wherever they go, their identity is enriched by this indirect title, signifying respect and recognition.

For Christian parents, it is customary to present the child in their church for dedication 40 days after birth. This occasion is marked with great celebration. A senior woman, often a deaconess (depending on the church's denomination), carries the child in her arms while the parents, well-wishers, and family members dance behind her as they approach the altar. The pastor, as a formality, publicly announces the child's name before performing the anointing and blessing with oil or water. The child is then handed back to the parents as a dedicated child of God.

In many African churches, the child is customarily handed over to the father after the dedication, possibly reflecting his role as the head of the family and primary provider. From that moment, it becomes the parents' responsibility to ensure the child's needs are met. For those who value education, this responsibility may extend to enrolling the child in nursery school as early as one year old.

Parents must ensure that all admission forms are completed accurately, providing the correct names, as these records serve as the foundation for the child's future development. This initial foundation, much like the base of a mansion, is pivotal in shaping the child's future achievements and identity.

CHAPTER FIVE

REPEATING ONE'S NAME

Variety in life is a creation of the Lord. He brings forth light from darkness and land from the ocean. Evidently, God possesses an appreciation for variety, as shown in His creation of fish for the water and animals of various sizes, from the smallest insect to the majestic elephant coexisting in the forest. He also recognised that the sky needed inhabitants, leading to the creation of assorted birds to fill the air.

According to both the Bible and the Holy Quran, human beings were created in the image of the living God from sand. To animate this sand form, God simply breathed life into its nostrils, transforming the clay figure into a living being. So pleased was He with His creation that He rested on the seventh day to observe the functioning of the beings He had made.

How, then, did humanity develop differences in colour, religion, language, and character? Both the Bible and the Quran recount that Jesus Christ and Prophet Muhammad (S.A.W) originated from the same region, spoke the same language, and dressed similarly, as they belonged to the same tribe. It is possible that humanity initially existed in one colour and one location. However, as people embarked on separate journeys in pursuit of better futures, environmental factors influenced their evolution. Those who ventured into colder climates evolved lighter complexions, while those who remained in hotter, forested regions of Africa developed darker or chocolate-toned skin. Research suggests that the Middle East is likely the cradle of humanity, and the natural complexion of the first humans in this region remained consistent.

The origin of humanity might have occurred in areas such as India, Egypt, and Iran, as suggested by archaeological findings. Egyptian mummies, buried thousands of years ago, continue to be unearthed, serving as evidence of humanity's early existence. These findings prompt us to ponder: where was the Garden of Eden located, what did Adam and Eve look like, and what were the complexions of their children?

The original Jews likely shared a similar external appearance with the original Arabs. Historical records reveal that their vocal and intolerant nature led to their displacement, forcing them to emigrate to various parts of the world. One wonders whether, had some of them been resettled in Africa, their God-given attributes of resilience and determination might have contributed to the development of the continent, preventing it from being labelled as a *dark continent* by Europeans during their expeditions.

From the Middle East, people migrated northwards, gradually developing lighter complexions, while those who moved southwards became darker or chocolate-toned. Environmental factors dictated the food they ate and the farming practices they adopted, influenced by what the climate permitted. In colder regions, necessity compelled innovation; for example, the harsh European winters required the invention of shoes to protect feet from freezing floors.

Why do we speak different languages? This question requires extensive empirical examination and a series of theses to substantiate various outcomes. What intrigues me most as an individual is why the phonetics of English spoken in Nigeria differ from those of Ghana, despite both countries being on the same continent and having learned English from the same missionaries.

Two theoretical approaches attempted to explain why people sometimes fail to understand others speaking the same language. One is the influence of local attitudes and perceptions, while the other involves phonetic differences. For instance, English comedians often jest about the distinctive ways in which the Welsh, Scots, and Irish speak, and vice versa. What is particularly perplexing, however, is the experience of an African person introducing themselves to an English receptionist. When they state their name, they are often asked repeatedly to repeat it. This situation becomes even more frustrating when they attempt to simplify the process by spelling their name. Unless they use the aviation-approved spelling codes, their efforts may be in vain.

This difficulty is not always accidental. In some instances, individuals deliberately feign misunderstanding to ridicule or dismiss others. Such behaviour can be both disheartening and discriminatory.

To mitigate these challenges, information technology has introduced standardised formats for resolving pronunciation and spelling issues. For example, the integration of date-of-birth verification in computational systems has eased the process of identifying individuals and has eliminated prolonged disputes, saving time and effort.

Despite these advancements, many people remain steadfast in preserving their cultural identity, including the names they give their children. Not everyone opts for foreign, Biblical, or Islamic names. Some individuals take great pride in their heritage, traditions, and virtues, insisting on passing these on to their descendants. This is particularly true of the Yoruba people, who name their children in ways that reflect their cultural upbringing. Names often begin with *Olúwa* (meaning God), *Ọlá* (meaning wealth), or *Adé* (meaning crown). Names that begin with *Adé*, for instance, indicate royal lineage. The Yoruba carefully consider family history and traditions when naming their children.

However, in environments where bias persists–such as dealing with a receptionist who harbours prejudice based on your appearance, race, or name–one might encounter deliberate attempts to provoke frustration. This could be a strategy to label you as impatient, rude, or unsuitable for some opportunities. Such situations may stem from phonetic misunderstandings but are sometimes rooted in intentional discrimination.

Thankfully, advancements in information technology have significantly reduced these challenges, if not eradicated them entirely. The resolution of these issues forms the focus of the next chapter.

CHAPTER SIX

INVENTION OF INFORMATION TECHNOLOGY

When I was studying in the United Kingdom some years ago, pursuing Business Studies at Woolwich Polytechnic in the 1970s, I noticed a trend among many women married to my cousins and friends. They were studying Data Processing, which was then a highly sought-after field. Companies were increasingly adopting it to manage how data was gathered, stored, and used in implementing wage structures for large organisations.

Data Processing involves maintaining detailed records of individual employees within a company, as well as those working for contractors executing projects on the company's behalf. The machines used for processing this data were enormous, occupying a significant portion of the buildings leased by these companies. These machines were heavily guarded to prevent unauthorised access. Strict measures were in place to protect against potential disruptions that could be caused by individuals with the expertise to manipulate or sabotage operations.

Life is a continuous process, evolving and transitioning from one stage to another. As a result, people, families, communities, and organisations must progress to reflect these changes. Nations that fail to adapt are often labelled as poor because they have not responded proactively and positively to the evolving needs of their populations.

Throughout history, there have been individuals who devoted their time and resources to improving humanity through research, investigations, and innovation. Their efforts to develop preventive measures and cures for health challenges have been recognised as invaluable services to humanity. These breakthroughs, when successful, have transformed the way we live today. They have shaped our lives and provided the means to protect our children from contagious diseases such as cholera, chickenpox, mpox, and poliomyelitis.

While their primary motivation may have been a genuine desire to make a significant impact on the human race, some may have had the secondary intention of profiting from their innovations in the long run. In many instances, however, they gained no tangible benefits from their work. Yet, their contributions have immortalised their names in history, celebrated in archives as pioneers whose discoveries have shaped the course of humanity.

When information technology began to influence human activities, it was prohibitively expensive at its inception. However, as demand grew, production intensified, leading to a rapid and gradual decline in prices. Over time, these technologies became accessible to the middle class. Today, it is almost unimaginable to consider how life would have been without mobile phones, iPads, desktop computers, laptops, and other gadgets too numerous to mention.

Some time ago, I was travelling on one of the London Underground trains when a gentleman boarded the coach at Stratford station, pushing a child in a pushchair. The child, who appeared to be between one and two years old, was handed a mobile phone by his father. To my astonishment, the child began navigating the phone with ease, searching for his favourite children's programmes.

At one point, the mobile phone accidentally slipped from the child's hands. When the father retrieved it, he decided not to return it. Chaos ensued. The child began screaming at the top of his lungs, struggling as though he wanted to escape from the pushchair by any means necessary. To avoid further disruption, the father had no choice but to return the mobile phone to the child. The moment the phone was back in his hands, peace and tranquillity were restored in the coach.

This incident illustrates that even at such a tender age, children value the use of information technology. For the child, watching videos on the mobile phone was not merely a privilege but something he regarded as his right.

Beyond entertainment, mobile phones serve a wide array of practical functions. They are used for making calls to relatives and friends, reporting updates to employers or colleagues, and amending erroneous information in reports during work hours. They enable users to request leave due to health issues, purchase goods online, and conduct banking transactions. Mobile phones have become indispensable tools for cashless transactions, allowing users to pay for items in shops or online and facilitating entry and exit at train stations by automatically deducting fares.

When used effectively, mobile phones place us firmly in a cashless world, eliminating the need to carry cash or even a bank card. Additionally, they help users navigate unfamiliar places without needing directions from others. From checking messages on WhatsApp to scrolling through Facebook, TikTok, Instagram, and other platforms, mobile phones have become constant companions for people of all ages, seen in their hands even as they walk the streets.

The challenges posed by how people use mobile phones and the dangers associated with these behaviours will be explored in another chapter. However, the example of the child described earlier demonstrates the profound impact technology has had on our modern lives.

Due to advancements in information technology, most office jobs are now performed on desktop computers within the workplace. During the Covid-19 pandemic, with its devastating effects on individuals and the economy, people were granted the unprecedented privilege of working from home. This arrangement meant that some employees attended their offices only once or twice a week. This shift was adopted to safeguard people and minimise the spread of the disease through physical contact and shared facilities.

The era of handwritten letters and memos was superseded by the advent of typewriters, which eventually fell into obsolescence. Handwriting gave way to the efficiency of typewriters, though these devices posed challenges, particularly their cumbersome nature when required in multiple locations. Researchers and developers dedicated to enhancing workplace technology persisted in their efforts, annually unveiling new models aimed at creating quieter and more efficient work environments.

The introduction of mobile phones significantly reduced reliance on landline telephones, which were limited to home or office use. To address accessibility, the government permitted the Post Office to install distinctive red-painted phone boxes along streets for public use. Mobile phones, however, revolutionised communication. Compact and portable, they could be held in one hand or carried in a pocket, allowing users to make calls anywhere, provided the battery remained functional. Despite their benefits, mobile phones brought with them certain challenges and dangers, which will be explored in another chapter.

The advent of iPads further expanded technological horizons, enabling users to access networks such as Facebook, WhatsApp, TikTok, and Instagram at any time and from anywhere. Computers, however, remained the cornerstone of office operations. They allowed users to draft letters, print documents, and transfer memos between colleagues for necessary actions. Email emerged as the fastest medium for disseminating information within workplaces, enabling management to communicate seamlessly with individual employees or entire teams. Notifications appeared simultaneously on multiple devices, ensuring a quiet and focused work environment where employees regularly checked for updates.

Laptops soon joined the wave of technological advancement, offering unprecedented portability. Lightweight and compact, laptops can be carried in a bag or held by hand, making them a versatile tool for modern professionals. It was common to see workers using laptops on buses, underground trains, or even during long-haul flights. To facilitate uninterrupted productivity for travellers, trains were equipped with network access and power outlets, allowing users to work seamlessly during their journeys.

The trajectory of information technology continues to evolve, driven by relentless research and development. The manufacturers remain in fierce competition, consistently unveiling innovative solutions to meet the demands of a dynamic and ever-changing digital landscape. One can only speculate about the breakthroughs that lie ahead.

CHAPTER SEVEN
YOUR FAMILY TREE

It often seems magical when I watch a presenter on television assisting individuals who have become celebrities in their professions or careers–such as comedians, actors, or sports personalities–trace their family origins back through many generations. I have witnessed presenters taking such individuals to locations where their great-grandparents once lived when they first arrived in the United Kingdom. This is often possible when relevant documentary evidence exists to trace the movement of early family members from house to house, town to town, job to job, and region to region.

Family trees are traced using birth certificates and marriage registry records. These documents reveal details such as parentage, marriages, the dates and locations of these events, and where the ceremonies took place. In some cases, family connections have been traced back as far as fifteen generations, often leading to remote locations in Russia or the Caribbean Islands in the West Indies. Many developed countries have designated offices, housing archives, and libraries of documents meticulously stored. These archives are managed by specialised personnel trained to retrieve the records and explain their historical significance to those making inquiries.

What the curator requires most are your name, your parents' names, your date of birth, and your parents' dates of birth. When the archive is accessed, the file often reveals the location of your birth and whether your parents were citizens of the country or migrants, including the date they arrived. It may also disclose details of their professions or careers, whether as restaurant attendants or construction workers, as these occupations were frequently well-documented.

Furthermore, if there are any criminal records, such as offences involving rape, burglary, or shoplifting, these are typically included in a designated column. Such records would detail the trial proceedings and the judgments pronounced in a court of law.

I recall how things were when I was growing up in the 1940s and 1950s. During that time, there were no registry offices to record births, deaths, or marriages. Instead, some parents recorded the birth of their children by writing the details on the walls of their living rooms, which we then referred to as parlours. The method was simple: using charcoal from burnt wood or planks, they would write something like, 'The wife of so-and-so had a baby boy (or girl) on such-and-such a date.' These inscriptions were prominently displayed on the sitting room wall, visible to all visitors.

At the time the record was made, the child often had not yet been named, as naming ceremonies typically took place on the eighth day after birth. Consequently, the mother's name became the reference point for identifying the child. This informal method was how many of us came to know the year, month, and date of our birth, although details such as the time and precise place of birth were often omitted.

Each wife typically had her own room with her children, depending on the number of children she bore. It was, therefore, customary for women to systematically record their children's birth dates on the walls of their bedrooms.

Thankfully, Western education and civilisation introduced us to more modern and reliable methods of record-keeping. In Africa generally, and Nigeria in particular, initiatives were introduced to establish birth and death registries in each local government area as well as marriages to maintain records of vital statistics. In the early days of these initiatives, the documents used for registration consisted of duplicated forms: the original copy was given to the registrant, while the carbon copy was stored in the office.

However, this system had its challenges. Climate issues such as storms, floods, and heavy rainfall, or incidents like office break-ins, workers' strikes, and even arson, often led to the destruction or loss of these vital records. We witnessed instances where strikes by workers protesting against unfavourable conditions resulted in offices being vandalised or burnt down, leaving important documents scattered on the streets or floating in rivers.

In developed countries, systems for record-keeping were established much earlier. For example, in England and Wales, the General Registry Office (GRO) was founded in July 1837. To trace one's ancestry further back, one would need to consult parish records. Over time, the legal framework expanded to include civil partnerships, granting legal recognition to same-sex unions and enabling the adoption of children within such families.

These developments have been meticulously documented by the General Registry Office, which also manages local archives and national archives to assist individuals in researching their family history.

How do we trace our family tree in Africa? Often, we rely solely on the elderly members of the family, who may have some knowledge of our family history. However, their accounts cannot always be trusted or relied upon absolutely, as age-related conditions like dementia may impair their memories, affecting their ability to recall events from their youth or early adulthood accurately. Without written records on paper, such narratives are susceptible to errors–whether through addition or omission–sometimes unintended but due to lapses in judgement.

It is almost certain that our forefathers were not born in the places we currently inhabit. Humanity has always been a migratory species, traversing the globe in search of opportunities, aspirations, and survival. In recent times, the term *Japa* has gained currency in Nigeria, symbolising the desperation of citizens to leave the country in pursuit of greener pastures. This desperation stems from an economic downturn that has rendered even the assurance of a day's meal a luxury for many. Consequently, some people resort to extreme measures, disregarding the rule of law and embracing a *do-or-die* mentality to escape the bleak realities of home.

I have heard and read about people selling everything they have worked for over six decades to finance emigration. Many borrow from banks and friends or liquidate their properties to sponsor their children's education at universities in the United Kingdom and Canada. A striking example is one of the vice-presidential candidates in the 2023 presidential elections, who, despite owning a university in Nigeria, sent his daughter to study abroad. This illustrates the lengths to which even those in power will go to secure better educational opportunities for their children, often starting as early as nursery school.

For those unable to meet the requirements for legal travel, the situation is even more dire. Some people die while attempting perilous journeys through the Sahara Desert en route to Libya and beyond. Travelling on foot without access to medical care or food supplies, they face an array of dangers, including attacks by wild animals, marauders, dehydration, and sheer exhaustion. Countless bodies are left by the roadside, abandoned to become skeletal remains or to be devoured by wildlife.

One poignant story tells of a young woman who embarked on such a journey without informing her parents, save for a brother who was privy to her plans. After some days, her mobile phone fell silent as its battery drained. Tragically, she collapsed and died along the way, with no identification or next-of-kin details to facilitate notification in the event of an emergency. Her family was left in anguish, unaware of her fate.

CHAPTER EIGHT

ARGUMENT ABOUT AGE SENIORITY

In societies where records of births and deaths are properly documented, maintained, and regularly updated as a matter of regulation, disputes regarding seniority among individuals are virtually eliminated. Each person's date, month, and year of birth, as recorded on their birth certificate, can be presented and verified if needed. However, when claims about one's age cannot be substantiated with authentic physical evidence, room is left for speculation and doubt.

When I was growing up, I observed instances where people who were slightly older than us would argue, sometimes to the point of physical altercations, over who was older. Neither party would accept the other's claims, often suspecting that the other was exaggerating their age to assert seniority. This contention was further compounded by its lack of tangible benefit beyond perceived superiority.

Historically, age groups in towns were categorised and given names to denote individuals born within three years. The disparity in maturity and experience between a child born three years ago and a newborn is apparent to anyone. Yet these groups adhered to longstanding cultural and traditional practices that have been observed for decades. Members of the same age group would unite under a common identity, forming what could be likened to a social trademark.

During significant social events such as the *Ojúde Oba*–an annual festival in Ìjèbú Òde celebrated on the third day after the Muslim festival of Eid-el-Kabir–Ileya, or local occasions like the Coronation Anniversary or *Ìwòyè Day* in Àgó-Ìwòyè, age groups would participate enthusiastically. These events involve funfairs, where members wear identical fabrics tailored in similar styles to foster a sense of unity and camaraderie.

However, there have been instances where people attempted to distance themselves from their assigned age groups due to personal assumptions of superiority. I recall a particular case of a man who believed his wealth, influence, or physical robustness placed him above his natural age group. He sought to align himself with the next senior age bracket, presuming his stature would earn him their acceptance. Despite his efforts, his application to join the senior group was rejected. His natural age group, feeling slighted by his behaviour, retaliated by enforcing punitive measures as per the group's established rules.

In one notable instance, they gathered in front of his family home to publicly denounce him, an act designed to humiliate him. Additionally, they seized a personal belonging–perhaps a sheet or similar item–and required him to pay the rightful owner as a form of restitution for his defiance. Such incidents reflect the complex interplay of cultural expectations, personal ambition, and communal regulation within these social structures.

Africa is often labelled the *undeveloped continent* because its governments have largely failed to use the God-given natural resources bestowed upon them. These resources, which could serve as tools to enhance the quality of life, ensure the security of lives and property, and provide comfort for the continent's inhabitants, remain underutilised. From the era of leaders such as Mobutu Sese Seko of the Republic of Congo, Robert Mugabe of Zimbabwe, General Sani Abacha of Nigeria, and the deposed president of Gambia, the political elite have consistently lacked genuine plans to develop their nations or equitably distribute resources for the benefit of their citizens. Instead, this class has perpetuated a cycle of poverty and suffering for the most vulnerable in society.

An illustrative example of this failure is seen in Nigeria's 10th Senate, where each Senator purchased an SUV worth ₦156 million. When questioned about such extravagance amidst prevailing economic hardships, one Senator, speaking on behalf of his colleagues, defended the expenditure, citing Nigeria's non-motorable roads and pervasive insecurity. Ironically, these issues–poor infrastructure and insecurity–fall squarely within the purview of the very lawmakers tasked with eradicating them through comprehensive budgeting and governance.

Across Africa, misplaced priorities often extend to the cultural and social spheres. In informal gatherings, it is not uncommon to hear arguments rooted in age seniority, with phrases such as, 'Don't you know I'm older than you?' or boasts about parental wealth. Such remarks, however, betray a lack of intellectual depth. After all, age is determined by when one enters the world, an occurrence beyond human control. Similarly, our departures will happen at varied times, under circumstances unique to each individual.

Indeed, even the concept of twin births demonstrates the arbitrary nature of age differences. There are documented cases where twins were born minutes apart, while others report gaps of days. For example, I once read about a mother whose twins were born three days apart. Remarkably, both children were delivered in good health with no signs of physical deficiencies. This exceptional case reminds us of the boundless possibilities of divine intervention.

Furthermore, the reluctance of individuals to disclose their true date of birth in certain situations reveals another facet of societal dysfunction. In hospitals, some refrain from providing accurate dates, fearing that previous criminal records could be uncovered. Similarly, at police stations, suspects often withhold their real names or birth dates to avoid the consequences of their past transgressions, as modern systems expose a history of criminal activity.

Nigeria's political landscape exemplifies how such deceitful practices infiltrate even the highest levels of governance. Many politicians, despite winning elections, have been disqualified by courts following petitions. These appeals, submitted against results announced by the Independent National Electoral Commission (INEC), often reveal discrepancies in candidates' submitted birth dates or educational qualifications. It is not merely electoral malpractice or manipulation of figures at issue, but a chronic pattern of dishonesty. Cases of forged certificates and falsified documents continue to undermine the integrity of the political process.

These are some of the allegations that political opponents often use to file petitions of discontent when they lose an election to candidates who have already been declared winners after the conclusion of the polls. When reviewing such cases, the courts typically require substantial evidence as a basis for any judgement. The evidence needed usually includes the date of the election, which serves as the crux of the case, alongside other documentary proof to support their claims regarding the conduct of the election, alleged malpractices, or unjust transfer of results to the final announcement centre.

The significance of the date of any event lies in its role as the foundation upon which further arguments or claims are constructed. This foundation must be solid, as its stability often determines how robust the case will be and its ability to withstand scrutiny. Similarly, as the durability of a building depends on the strength of its foundation, so too does the integrity of an electoral petition rely on this fundamental element.

As the Bible teaches, 'The stone which the builders rejected has become the cornerstone.' In the same way, a tree requires a strong and solid stem to support its branches and to withstand the winds and storms that would otherwise topple it. Solid foundations, whether in architecture, nature, or legal arguments, are essential for enduring strength and stability.

CHAPTER NINE
AT EVERY RECEPTION

Every organisation, whether a manufacturing firm, office building, or service provider, irrespective of size, must designate an open space at the entrance of the building exclusively for the receptionist. Receptionists serve as the first point of contact for visitors and are tasked with ensuring that only those with a legitimate reason–such as attending an interview or responding to a verbal or written invitation–are permitted entry. Maintenance subcontractors, similarly, must be authorised before carrying out their assignments.

In cases of written invitations, visitors are required to present documentary evidence that unequivocally proves their bona fide invitation. For verbal invitations, the host must be contacted to confirm awareness of the visitor's arrival. If confirmed, the host is expected to personally escort the visitor to their designated location. This system mitigates unauthorised access and prevents potential security breaches by people loitering around the premises. As the saying goes, prevention is better than cure.

This process underscores the importance of precise scheduling, particularly in employment scenarios. Applicants invited for interviews must adhere strictly to the stated date, time, and venue. Candidates are often grouped by the interview panel's chosen criteria–such as alphabetical order or on a first-come, first-served basis. Any oversight in remembering the interview details could lead to missed opportunities, which, in competitive job markets, are unlikely to be rescheduled.

It is unfortunate that many candidates have lost valuable opportunities simply due to forgetting interview dates or confusing schedules with other commitments. In such circumstances, failing to prioritise the interview can result in irrevocable losses. Employment applications are inherently competitive; thus, securing an interview invitation is a significant achievement that should be treated with utmost importance.

The receptionist's primary role is to warmly welcome all visitors and direct them to the appropriate office floor or department relevant to their visit. However, the receptionist's responsibilities are clearly delineated. They are not authorised to provide detailed answers to certain enquiries or disclose specific information, even if accessible via their computer systems. Instead, they guide visitors to the relevant personnel or department for assistance.

Typically, the receptionist will inform visitors that any outstanding questions will be addressed by their host upon meeting. This clear division of duties–knowing where one role ends and another begins–reflects the principle of division of labour, ensuring organisational efficiency and clarity in responsibilities.

The receptionist is not allowed to answer some questions nor allowed to give out some information despite the fact that the information could be on the computer in front of them, they may be able to direct you to the persons or section that deal with the matter directly. The common answer to some question from the receptionist is that your host would discuss all issues with you when you meet and you are free to ask him any question. There is always line of demarcation of duty, when the assignment of A ends and that of B commences. That is what they call division of labour.

When you attempt to bypass the reception forcefully, you can justifiably be arrested, labelled as a terrorist, and handed over to the police as a suspect for interrogation. Your background will then be thoroughly investigated to uncover any previous criminal records, determining whether you have been involved in serious criminal activities.

In modern establishments, trained security personnel often act as receptionists to deter unauthorised individuals from attempting to gain access. This practice ensures that only those with legitimate reasons or formal invitations are encouraged to enter. It is especially crucial during a time when terrorists seek every opportunity to infiltrate buildings or their external surroundings.

Such individuals may use mobile phones or cameras to capture images of a building's layout as part of their plans. If any suspicious activity is detected, the security team must prepare a comprehensive report, including the date and time of the incident, the areas photographed, and detailed descriptions of the individual involved. This documentation is critical, as the police may already be on alert for someone matching that description.

The recording of dates and times has become a central aspect of security planning, ensuring society is better equipped to prevent harmful incidents.

CHAPTER TEN

ONLINE USES OF DATE OF BIRTH

The value and utility of mobile phones have made them indispensable gadgets, so essential that they defy full description and surpass comparison with any other innovation in modern technology. We now use mobile phones anytime and anywhere, regardless of the hour or how remote the location is. The connectivity provided by mobile networks has transformed the United Kingdom into a small, virtually connected space, creating what feels like magic to users like me. The sheer number of uses and purposes for which a mobile phone can be employed is astonishing.

Take communication, for example. The need for physical presence during conversations has been supplanted by mobile phones, enabling privacy and convenience in an unparalleled manner. Platforms like WhatsApp have revolutionised interaction, allowing users to connect effortlessly with contacts for conversations, text exchanges, and media sharing. What is particularly impressive is the affordability–beyond your subscription fees, costs are minimal. If you exceed your data usage, you are promptly alerted, giving you the chance to manage consumption and avoid additional charges. Though advertised as *free,* it is wise to remember the monthly charges or pay-as-you-go top-ups that enable such convenience.

In this digital era, it is almost inconceivable to require in-person presence for routine tasks like bookings. Today, numerous transactions and daily activities can be completed effortlessly via mobile phones, eliminating the need to leave your home or office. Gone are the days of seeking public telephone boxes or trudging half a mile to find one installed by the Post Office. Instead, your mobile phone is a portable powerhouse–ready to pull from your pocket or bag at a moment's notice. Calls can be made anytime, even while walking down the street or travelling on public transport, provided consideration is given to fellow passengers by keeping noise levels low.

Mobile phones also facilitate interactions with essential services such as healthcare providers. For instance, you can book appointments with your General Practitioner (GP) or receive text reminders about upcoming consultations. Similarly, any changes to a scheduled appointment–perhaps due to the specialist's unavailability–can be promptly communicated. It is now common to wake up, ring your GP's office as soon as it opens, and secure an appointment within minutes. The same applies when requesting medication from your registered pharmacy. Upon contacting their receptionist, you will typically be asked to confirm your name, followed by more specific details such as your date of birth. This allows your information to be retrieved instantly, ensuring efficient service delivery, whether it is confirming an appointment or arranging for medication collection.

Time, now more precious than ever, is saved significantly through online conveniences. For instance, banking has undergone a dramatic transformation, especially among younger generations who rarely visit physical branches. Most transactions–be it transferring money, topping up electricity and gas meters, or paying for travel–can now be handled seamlessly via mobile apps. Even public transport payments, traditionally made with debit cards, have evolved to support mobile apps for check-ins and check-outs.

Retail transactions are equally simplified. Shops increasingly cater to customers who wish to scan, select, and pay for their items through apps or debit cards, bypassing traditional checkouts entirely. When observing the multitude of apps on some users' phones, I often marvel at their ability to navigate and manage such a vast array of options.

Bank interactions, too, have adapted to ensure security in the face of rising fraud and scams. When calling your bank to request information or seek account-related advice, the initial queries often include your name, account number, date of birth, and sometimes even your postcode. These steps reassure the bank that they are speaking to the rightful account holder while providing you with the necessary assistance.

Registering for admission to a college or university has become a routine task that is now predominantly conducted online. Applicants can effortlessly complete their admission forms and pay the necessary school fees via the Internet, anytime, and from anywhere. Many colleges and universities have also adapted to online teaching methods, delivering education either in group sessions or one-on-one via platforms such as Zoom, depending on the institution's protocols or specific circumstances. Consequently, some students may visit their campuses no more than five times throughout their entire four-year academic tenure, with the entirety of their learning and coursework conducted virtually.

The impact of online advancements is not limited to education alone. There was a notable political controversy in Nigeria not long ago involving a judge who, while abroad, delivered a decision on a case he had presided over before travelling. Nigerian politicians, supported by unscrupulous, profit-driven lawyers, vehemently protested, claiming the judge lacked jurisdiction to pass judgement while outside the country. The dissent was as loud as barking dogs, with critics metaphorically kicking dust into the sky. However, their appeal against the judgement's circumstances was dismissed by a higher court, which upheld the provisions of the Constitution of the Federal Republic of Nigeria (1999, as amended). The Constitution allows for judgements to be issued from any location worldwide, provided the case has been duly heard and concluded. This incident exemplifies the pervasive role of online tools in our everyday lives.

Commerce has also been profoundly influenced by online innovation. Online shopping has boosted sales and profitability for supermarkets and shop owners, expanding their customer base beyond physical footfall. It is now common to see delivery personnel on bicycles or motorbikes, carrying branded bags from companies like Just Eat, KFC, Ocado, and others. Meals ordered online are swiftly delivered to customers' doorsteps, hot and fresh, thanks to seamless processes. Customers simply place their orders by phone, providing details such as their name, address, and bank information. Payments are automatically deducted, and delivery times are assured.

Furthermore, supermarket delivery vans are now ubiquitous, ensuring bulk orders reach customers at their homes or workplaces promptly. These vans operate 24/7, covering even the remotest corners of the country. Supermarkets like Sainsbury's, Asda, Tesco, Ocado, Iceland, and Amazon have mastered these delivery systems. They guarantee in their promotional materials that items ordered online by midday will be delivered on the same day. In a competitive marketplace, their ability to fulfil such promises directly influences customer loyalty. The range of items delivered varies greatly, from food and fresh produce to clothing on rolling rails, potted flowers, and even building materials–some of which are assured delivery within 12 hours of purchase.

Hospitals, too, have embraced digitalisation in their communication practices. Traditional methods of sending test results via postal letters have largely been replaced with more instantaneous messaging systems. With 99 per cent of patients providing mobile phone numbers and email addresses for communication, hospitals can now efficiently send notifications or updates. Messages are dispatched via email or phone-based messengers, eliminating delays and the need for envelopes or postal stamps. In urgent cases, digital correspondence ensures that patients receive the necessary information promptly and securely, aligning with the demands of modern healthcare.

Regardless of the method adopted, your details must include your name and date of birth, as these serve as primary points of reference. For instance, when a bystander is stopped by the police–perhaps as the driver of a suspected stolen vehicle or in an area where a crime has recently occurred–the first thing officers will typically ask for is your name. However, they are unlikely to believe the name you initially provided, as they often assume suspects may be evasive in an attempt to avoid detention.

The police will record the name you provide and consider you a suspect, using your details in radio communications with other officers to inform them that you are in custody. Upon arrival at the police station, the focus often shifts to your date of birth. This piece of information is crucial for verifying your identity, checking for any previous aliases, and ascertaining whether you have a history of criminal records. At times, officers may also take a DNA sample to trace your past activities.

It is only when your correct date of birth is obtained that investigations can proceed in line with the purpose for which you were taken into custody. Additionally, fingerprinting provides another method for tracing a suspect's criminal history. However, even when a suspect is firmly implicated in a crime and the case proceeds to court, it is important to remember that a suspect is considered innocent until proven guilty by a court of law. As the adage goes, 'Suspicion is not a crime unless it is proven beyond reasonable doubt.' If found guilty, the suspect is sentenced according to the legal mandates prescribed by the country's criminal laws.

In Nigeria, facilities for incarcerating offenders are no longer referred to as *prisons* but have been renamed *Correctional Centres*. However, the extent to which these institutions fulfil their corrective mandate is a matter of ongoing controversy–a debate best left for another time.

A recent case illustrates some peculiarities within the Nigerian system. A cross-dresser was convicted of the offence of scattering money on the ground, leading to people trampling on the currency–an act deemed criminal. Following his arrest and subsequent trial, he was found guilty and sentenced to serve a specified term in a correctional centre. Later, reports emerged through a recorded media interview in which he revealed that instead of being transported to the correctional centre after the court proceedings, he was taken to a special lodge and accommodated outside the correctional facility.

This revelation sparked widespread disbelief, epitomised by the phrase, 'Wonders will never end in Nigeria.' It suggests that the correctional centre in question neither recorded nor stored any details about him, including fingerprints, which could be referenced in the future for any further legal or investigative purposes. Incidents like this underscore Nigeria's unique approach to law enforcement and criminal justice–a system that defies comparison with those of other nations.

NIGERIA MY COUNTRY.

CHAPTER ELEVEN
PLANTS AND FLOWERS ARE PLANTED IN DATES

A nation's development cannot be measured by the flashy cars on its roads, the extravagant vehicles in the garages of the wealthy, towering skyscrapers that pierce the sky, or lavish parties where individuals flaunt wads of the highest denominations–₦1000 notes–stuffed in *Ghana-must-go* bags, tossing cash at musicians who lavish them with hollow social titles. To the educated and well-cultured citizens who possess integrity and are committed to the nation's progress, such behaviour serves only to ridicule efforts at genuine development.

True civilisation lies in providing security for citizens and safeguarding their properties. It requires a nation to meticulously document its innovations and ensure they serve the welfare of its people. In Nigeria, we have witnessed tragic images of pensioners wandering, aimlessly and uncertain of where to claim their hard-earned entitlements after establishments are liquidated and organisations sold off to private interests. These individuals, who dedicated 45 years of mandatory service or reached the retirement age 60, are left destitute–roaming the streets like lost souls, sometimes succumbing to the strain of chasing elusive pensions. They are denied the opportunity to enjoy the fruits of their labour, a cruel injustice to those who once served their motherland.

In contrast, pensioners in the United Kingdom should be considered. Here, offices specifically designed for retired workers–both civilian and military–are established within local government facilities. These offices, furnished to high standards, welcome retirees who provide documentation to register as members. Within these spaces, retirees can gather, socialise, and enjoy affordable beverages, including tea, chocolate, beer, or wine–subsidised to foster a sense of community.

Social interaction, as recognised by medical research, is a cornerstone of good health and longevity, promoting laughter, conversation, and connection that lead to happiness and vitality. The United Kingdom exemplifies this ethos, with carefully planned environments and homes–whether private or council-owned–designed by qualified architects. Experts review and refine these plans, ensuring any necessary amendments are integrated into the final designs. Although occasional disasters occur due to human error or oversight, deliberate negligence–such as skimping on materials like iron rods or cement in construction–is unacceptable. Adding floors to structures without the necessary reinforcements is considered criminal and punishable by years of imprisonment.

Unfortunately, in Africa, such greed and selfishness among contractors often result in catastrophic building collapses, claiming innocent lives. Daily reports of such tragedies emerge from cities like Lagos, Enugu, Bayelsa, and Abuja. These incidents stem from inadequate supervision and the reckless execution of contracts, with little regard for safety or ethical standards. While penalties exist for contractors found guilty of such negligence, they fail to prevent the persistent loss of lives. A robust system of accountability and oversight is imperative to curb this epidemic and safeguard the future.

Every space within certain areas of the United Kingdom is adorned with trees and flowering plants that not only enhance the beauty of these places but also provide shade over the ground and a refreshing environment for those who recreate or take leisurely walks beneath them. These natural features offer residents in the area a cool, airy atmosphere, while even the surroundings of office buildings are often landscaped with trees that cast their shadows on the ground. These shaded areas provide fresh air and a retreat where workers can relax and engage in conversation during their breaks or recess.

Some years ago, I worked on Kensington High Street, near the Commonwealth Secretariat within the Borough of Chelsea and Kensington in the West End. Along this stretch, there was a row of approximately 25 interconnected houses in need of renovation. These properties featured a long car park at the front, where residents and visitors could conveniently park their cars. Trees were planted to enhance the appeal of the compound, shading the buildings and providing a buffer from the main road's activity.

It was necessary to deliver building materials to the rear of the houses to facilitate the renovation process. However, the only feasible means of access involved demolishing one of the central houses in the compound, allowing trucks to transport materials to the contractors. Additionally, for construction to commence, one or two rows of trees in front of the houses had to be felled. It was at this point I learned a significant lesson about environmental stewardship in the United Kingdom: every planted tree has an official record.

The contractor hired to remove the trees needed explicit permission from the Chelsea and Kensington Town Hall, which governs the area. An application was submitted to the council, and shortly after that, a council official arrived, carrying a bundle of documents detailing the history of the trees. To my astonishment, the records included the names assigned to each tree, along with the exact dates they were planted and the company contracted for the planting. It amazed me that most trees lining London's streets and parks have official documentation recording their planting dates, months, and years. This revelation led me to conclude that meticulous record-keeping plays a pivotal role in the UK's development, with archives properly maintained for future reference.

In stark contrast, Nigeria has failed to document significant historical events adequately. Consider the Biafran War: an insurgent and conventional conflict whose dates of declaration and cessation are neither observed nationally nor recognised by state authorities. There is no annual remembrance for those who lost their lives, nor a formal platform for reflection on the lessons learned from that tragic chapter.

In the United Kingdom, by comparison, the end of the First and Second World Wars is marked with solemnity. Every 11th November, known as Remembrance Day, the Royal Family, politicians, and senior military officials lay wreaths to honour the fallen. The occasion serves not as a symbol of victory over the enemy but as a commemoration of sacrifice and loss. In the days leading up to this date, citizens, particularly the youths, engage in traditions such as lighting bangers to underline the enduring memory of those who gave their lives.

Meanwhile, in Nigeria, it is largely the directives of groups like IPOB (Indigenous People of Biafra) that force a semblance of remembrance through Monday's sit-at-home orders in states like Anambra and Ebonyi. Without these, the Biafran War might have faded entirely from collective memory. The younger generation lacks textbooks or curricula that document the war or its broader implications, leaving them bereft of historical perspective.

It is a national failing that records of events–whether as families or as a country–are not kept. The Bible teaches that God worked for six days to create the universe and rested on the seventh, demonstrating the importance of marking time. This divine example underscores the significance of preserving dates and records both on earth and in heaven.

CHAPTER TWELVE

TIME IS MONEY

Money is widely recognised as one of the most crucial assets in people's lives, though it is often considered secondary to good health. Nevertheless, money plays a significant role in sustaining human well-being and facilitating a means of livelihood. An individual who cannot afford to meet basic needs is often regarded by society as a burden on their family, community, and state.

In this context, money does not refer to amassing millions of pounds sterling or billions of naira in the bank, but rather the ability to fulfil daily necessities for oneself and one's family. These needs can be met either by working for an organisation or by pursuing a trade, thereby becoming self-employed. The ability to earn sufficient income to cater to one's daily requirements depends largely on the willingness to comply with assigned responsibilities, especially in formal employment, where little choice exists but to adhere to instructions. For those whose temperament does not accommodate being directed, self-employment offers an alternative–perhaps through running a retail shop or working as a tradesperson such as a mechanic operating a small roadside shop based on one's skills.

Why do we need money? Firstly, employment instils self-discipline, enforcing routines such as leaving for work in the morning, afternoon, or evening, depending on one's schedule. Secondly, it teaches individuals to follow the rules and regulations of an organisation. Thirdly, work provides an income that must be budgeted and prioritised wisely. Finally, it fosters habits such as socialising, punctuality, and engaging with others.

Life, however, is not a bed of roses. For some, life unfolds with ease–they acquire what they desire with minimal effort, exactly when and how they want it. At the opposite end of the spectrum, others toil relentlessly, often without achieving their goals. The saying, 'All the fingers on one hand are not equal', offers profound insight into the inherent inequalities of life.

Connections and family background often determine access to opportunities. For instance, we frequently observe students of average academic performance securing lucrative employment shortly after graduation, courtesy of their networks. Meanwhile, exceptionally bright graduates with top grades often struggle to find roles offering more than the government-mandated minimum wage.

On the streets, one can observe the stark disparities in living conditions. Some people drive or are chauffeured in luxurious vehicles, while others queue at food banks, waiting for free meals long past breakfast hours. The meals they receive may not align with their preferences or what they might have chosen if circumstances allowed, but dire realities leave them with little choice. Yet, as the Bible reminds us, 'When there is life, there is hope.'

Time governs most human activities, including employment. Terms of employment are often outlined clearly, specifying hours of work, rates of pay, modes of payment, and contract duration–whether temporary or renewable–along with the conditions for renewal, which vary across organisations.

As highlighted elsewhere, time also features prominently in life's milestones. For example, when a child is born in a hospital, the attending nurse records the exact minute, hour, and month of birth. This documentation is essential when registering the child's date of birth after they are named. However, in some parts of Africa, birth registration often lacks such evidential documentation, enabling practices such as registering a child's birth without proper verification. This lack of transparency forms one of the fundamental roots of societal corruption.

When governments or large companies wish to sign a contract with another entity, whether another corporation or a government body, the date of the agreement is one of the most critical factors that the legal teams on both sides scrutinise. Such contracts must explicitly state when work will commence, the expected completion date, and, for construction-related projects–such as building houses or roads–when the project will be handed over for use, whether to tenants or the public.

Many of us obtain loans from banks for various projects or enter into mortgage agreements with lenders to purchase properties, either as family homes or business ventures. These contracts clearly outline the terms of payment and the duration of the agreement until its expiry.

A similar framework applies when purchasing a car on hire purchase. Typically, the longest hire purchase agreements for vehicles last four years. Any failure to comply with the terms of such agreements before the expiry date constitutes a breach of contract. This often results in adverse outcomes for the buyer, such as the repossession of the vehicle.

When I first arrived in the United Kingdom, I noticed that canned foods were labelled with both their production and expiration dates. Some items, like plastic-bottled milk, had short expiry periods of two weeks, while others extended to a year or more. Initially, I believed these dates were deliberately included to encourage consumers to purchase replacements, whether the product was used or not. I interpreted this approach as a means of sustaining production, thereby keeping workers employed and earning incomes.

Even borrowing a book from a public library involves a time-bound agreement. Each book comes with a designated borrowing period indicated on the attached tag. Librarians, as part of their professional responsibilities, verbally remind borrowers of the specific return date. This ensures the availability of the book for other borrowers who might have reserved it. Failure to return the book on time could result in a fine, serving as a penalty for breaching the terms of the borrowing agreement.

Advancements in information technology (IT) have significantly simplified many aspects of daily life. For instance, individuals familiar with mobile applications can easily check the arrival times of public transport buses at the nearest stop. This convenience allows users to plan their departure times more effectively, whether commuting to work, going shopping, or enjoying family outings. Such technological innovations eliminate the frustration of standing at bus stops, uncertain about the next bus' arrival.

The impact of technology extends further. When searching for specific information, tools like Google can guide you not only to the details of an event but also to its exact date, month, and even location. Such capabilities underscore the multifaceted ways innovation is transforming every dimension of human endeavour on a daily basis.

CHAPTER THIRTEEN

CHANGING THE CLOCK'S TIME

Religions have long taught us that everything in heaven and on earth was created by God and that, as it was over 60 million years ago, so, it shall remain for eternity. Questioning this theological premise is often considered blasphemous, with modern General Overseers, who lead church affairs, labelling dissenters as agents of Satan.

However, in reality, life is far from static. The media and researchers continually report discoveries and evolving events worldwide. For instance, television news often broadcasts the ongoing conflict between Israel and Gaza. Israel has retaliated against Gaza for killing over 1,300 citizens, many of whom were innocent children, within its territory. This conflict has since extended to involve Lebanon and Iran, both of whom are accused of supporting Gaza by sending bombs into Israel. Similarly, we witness Russia's destructive war on Ukraine, led by President Vladimir Putin, as he attempts to annex Ukraine back into Russian territory. Without televised reports of bombings and devastation, many would dismiss these atrocities, while others might label them as *fake news*.

In Africa, there is a common belief in some quarters that day breaks simultaneously across all regions, just as night falls uniformly. Yet, technology has revealed this to be false. In the United States of America, for instance, multiple states operate in different time zones. While it is 7 a.m. in one state, it might be 5 a.m. in another–a difference of one or more hours, determined to suit regional needs and codified into law.

The disparity extends globally. A flight from the United Kingdom to some airports in the United States typically takes five hours, yet the time difference between the two countries is six hours. These variations in time zones result from deliberate human calculations to address societal and economic demands.

Science has further demonstrated the vast differences in the animal kingdom. Animals differ not only in size but also in dietary preferences. For instance, elephants subsist on vegetation, whereas their *cousin*, the lion, is carnivorous and preys on other animals. Such contrasts highlight divergent survival instincts. Lions and tigers cannot endure prolonged hunger, needing frequent kills for sustenance. In contrast, camels can store food and water, allowing them to survive for months in arid conditions. While lions and tigers are predators, hunting relentlessly to survive, the mighty elephants and giraffes–despite their imposing size–graze gently as they search for sustenance.

Travelling the world offers further insights into humanity's dietary diversity. What one region considers a staple may be unfamiliar or even repellent to another. This aptly reflects the adage, 'One man's meat is another man's poison.'

October, the tenth month of the year, marks a time when authorities in certain countries adjust clocks by one hour backwards. This change, dictated by human decisions rather than natural forces, addresses the shortening of days as winter approaches. By contrast, in April, the clocks are set forward by an hour to maximise daylight. These adjustments aim to create a safer environment for schoolchildren, ensuring they commute to and from school in adequate daylight.

The welfare of children, often seen as future leaders, remains a core concern for governments and parents alike. Mothers, in particular, worry about their children's safety during early morning and late afternoon journeys. By law, children under nine years of age must be accompanied by a parent or an authorised adult when travelling to and from school. These regulations and the collective effort to adjust timeframes demonstrate a society's commitment to protecting its most vulnerable members.

It may present a hazardous obligation imposed by law on working-class parents, particularly in instances where both are employed, coupled with the mandatory requirement that children must attend school. If a child persistently misses school, the headteacher is obliged to report the matter to social services. These agencies may, in turn, involve the police, who are equipped to conduct prompt investigations, including visits to the family home, to uncover the circumstances contributing to the child's absence from school.

Persistent absenteeism is treated as a serious offence, with the law taking a stringent view of such occurrences. School authorities are often mandated to raise an alarm if there is suspicion surrounding a child's continued absence. Such alerts are usually forwarded to the police, who then investigate potential issues within the family, such as inadequate parental care or home instability, that could deter the child from attending school. Investigations may reveal various underlying factors, including a disjointed family dynamic where, despite living under the same roof, parents may lead separate lives. In some cases, the father may fail to fulfil his familial responsibilities, resulting in poverty or an inability to provide essentials like breakfast for the child–circumstances that may dampen the child's enthusiasm for school attendance. When such findings emerge, the police may direct the local council to provide financial support to the family to alleviate these challenges.

Child starvation is a particularly critical concern that governments in the United Kingdom are resolute in preventing. In instances where such neglect persists, the child may be removed from the family and placed under adoption or foster care, where they would receive sufficient care, often supplemented by financial aid from the council to support their well-being.

The police are also empowered to stop and question school-aged children found wandering during school hours. While the questioning is typically gentle, it can be probing enough to address any inconsistencies in the child's explanation. If the police find the child's account suspicious, they may accompany the child to their home to assess whether they are being neglected or left without adequate care. Cases of parental negligence can lead to severe legal consequences, including the removal of children from their families by the council for adoption or foster placement. Such cases are not uncommon among African families residing in the UK.

Children themselves, in specific circumstances such as experiencing bullying or starvation, may report their parents to the school welfare officer if these issues impact their behaviour or performance. Welfare officers will collect evidence from the child, including details such as the date and time of the incidents, along with physical proof like visible marks on the child's body. With the headteacher's approval, such cases are reported to social services, who may take up the matter directly or escalate it to the police for further investigation and appropriate action.

CHAPTER FOURTEEN
MEMORABLE DATES

As I have come to understand and adopted as part of my life philosophy, history is not made for anyone in heaven. History comprises events that occur to an individual after birth. While unborn in heaven, there is nothing to document as occurrences in a person's life. For some people, history may begin as early as during pregnancy. For instance, a foetus in the womb may develop complications leading to a miscarriage or stillbirth.

In Europe, once a wife, partner, or girlfriend is confirmed to be pregnant, medical tests are conducted to determine the baby's gender. As soon as the child's gender is identified, the couple begins deliberating on what to name the baby upon delivery. At this stage, the baby already has a name. Even if the pregnancy is lost, to the family, it is already a child, and the child's brief existence becomes part of the family's history.

Medical science has advanced significantly. Some foetuses, discovered during examinations to be positioned outside the mother's womb, have been surgically repositioned. This rare surgery allows the child to develop correctly. However, I am not convinced we perform similar procedures in Africa yet. Perhaps, one day, we shall catch up.

I recall a media report about a Nigerian medical doctor, trained in Nigeria but practising in the United States. During a routine examination, he discovered complications in a baby still in the womb. He performed a groundbreaking surgery, temporarily removing the baby from the womb, addressing the medical issues, and then returning the baby to the womb. The pregnancy culminated in the safe delivery of a healthy baby. This achievement was hailed as a world first.

When people say, 'Nigerians are brilliant', is not an exaggeration. I only wish that Nigeria's federal and state governments would invest in adequate infrastructure in our public hospitals. Doing so could reduce infant and maternal mortality rates by up to 85%. As it stands, the statistics for these deaths are catastrophic.

Nigerians possess the intellect and capability to provide medical care on par with their counterparts in the UK and USA. The passion is there, but they are hindered by a lack of proper equipment and conducive working environments. It is disheartening to read in national and international news about the abduction and murder of doctors in various parts of Nigeria. Even when ransoms are partially paid, both the person delivering the ransom and the kidnapped doctor often lose their lives.

One case that comes to mind is that of a Nigerian living in the United States who returned to Ile-Ife to invest in a hotel and farming business. He and a female staff member–a university student–were kidnapped. The family managed to gather money for ransom, sent via a motorcyclist, only for the motorcyclist to be killed after delivering the money. Both victims were also killed.

The prevailing insecurity in Nigeria has driven many enlightened citizens to flee the country in search of greener pastures. The government bears significant blame for this exodus. Countries such as the United Kingdom, United States, and Canada now reap the rewards of Nigeria's education system by benefiting from the expertise of Nigerian-trained doctors. Ironically, these same doctors would have flourished at home had conditions been more favourable.

Our political leaders set poor examples. They frequently travel abroad for medical treatment using state resources, demonstrating their lack of faith in the healthcare system they oversee. During his tenure, General Babangida regularly visited Germany for treatment, even for minor ailments. President Buhari made long and frequent visits to the United Kingdom for medical care, and President Bola Ahmed Tinubu has already made over three trips to the UK for similar purposes within his first year in office.

If such visits were documented and broadcast, we might find that some of the attending doctors abroad are Nigerians. This highlights the adage, 'The spirit is willing, but the flesh is weak.' No politician seems to care for the wellbeing of ordinary Nigerians. As long as they and their families can afford to travel abroad for treatment, their concerns for the nation's healthcare system end there.

Even parents who struggled to raise their children out of starvation and poverty are often unable to reap the fruits of their labour. At the first opportunity, young graduates vanish to what they refer to as *better countries* or *greener pastures,* where the infrastructure exists to support the skills they acquired at Nigerian universities. These host countries, however, often lack the manpower specialists they require and are forced to seek them from other nations. This situation echoes the adage: 'Those who have heads have no caps, and those who have caps have no heads.' Is this the destiny God has chosen for Nigeria, or is it a result of the mismanagement and theft of Nigeria's natural resources scattered across distant lands? Perhaps we should leave that for posterity to judge.

I am always fascinated when I read in newspapers or magazines about couples fortunate enough to have been married for over sixty years and remain living together as husband and wife. These couples often narrate their journey, recalling with clarity the first time they met and what attracted them to one another. They recount the details of their first outing, whether it was to a restaurant or a theatre, as well as the date of their engagement, who proposed first, and the events of their wedding day. Just last week, I read about a 105-year-old man and his 100-year-old wife, who had been married for 82 years, reminiscing about their romantic years together.

Such couples usually share the highlights of their relationship, showcasing the good times while carefully omitting the challenges and adversities that nearly tore them apart. They avoid recounting disloyal acts, conflicts, or moments of weakness, presenting themselves instead as what society calls the *perfect couple*. When I was growing up, there was a saying: 'When you laugh, people laugh with you; when you throw a party, people gather to eat, drink, and celebrate. But when circumstances turn bitter and you are left to cry, you cry alone. Others are too occupied with their problems to lend you comfort.'

Some days remain etched in memory–some for their joy, others for their sorrow. The loss of a loved one to illness, a tragic accident, or even the devastating effects of the COVID-19 pandemic leaves a lasting mark. No amount of time can erase these moments from the hearts of those left behind.

Similarly, the sudden breakdown of a marriage can leave wounds that refuse to heal. Imagine sharing your life with someone for over twenty years, only for them to suddenly declare, 'It's over.' Without prior warning or apparent signs of trouble, they pack their belongings and leave. Such an incident is deeply heartbreaking and impossible to forget.

Even a driver with years of experience can encounter an accident due to mechanical failure, human error, or the negligence of others. If the accident results in an injury that leaves a visible scar, each glance in the mirror serves as a reminder of that fateful day. While minor injuries might be joked about among friends, some experiences linger as permanent marks on both body and memory.

Parents occupy an irreplaceable role in our lives. They give us life, nurture us, and guide us towards a bright future. We may rebel against their guidance in our youth, believing it outdated or in conflict with the freedoms our friends appear to enjoy. However, it is often after their passing that we reflect on the wisdom of their words and the sacrifices they made. Many live with regret for having ignored or disrespected their parents, only realizing too late the depth of their loss.

I recall watching a video about an eagle in South Africa some years ago. It must have been a female eagle, which displayed a fiercely territorial nature, attacking anyone who inadvertently ventured near its domain. Its behaviour mirrored the harsh apartheid regime, indiscriminately hostile to all intruders, irrespective of their skin colour. Despite this, a man promised his neighbours he would befriend the bird–a declaration met with ridicule, as many believed it to be impossible.

Undeterred, the man observed the eagle's preferences and began leaving its favourite food in a designated spot each morning when the bird was absent. Over time, the eagle came to recognise him, associating the same figure in the same attire with its daily meal. One day, the man arrived as usual to deposit the food, unaware that the eagle was hiding nearby. As he walked away, the eagle flew down, landing on his shoulder. Terrified of being attacked, the man froze, only to realise that the bird was gazing at him with curiosity.

From that moment, a bond formed between them. The eagle began visiting the man's home twice a week, much to the amazement–and fear–of those who witnessed their interactions. This story serves as a powerful reminder that patience and persistence can transform even the most challenging situations.

CHAPTER FIFTEEN
THE RACE FOR TIME

The Olympic Games are held every four years and hosted by a different country each time. The event symbolises a universally organised competition for nations equipped with the required resources and facilities. The world governing body appoints the host country through a voting process. Athletes who perform exceptionally well during the games, as witnessed on television screens worldwide, are often celebrated for their remarkable achievements.

The 2012 London Olympics featured inspiring names that captivated audiences, such as Mo Farah and Usain Bolt. Their achievements earned them global recognition, not through prayers or devotion to any religion, but through relentless effort and rigorous preparation. Gone are the days when miracles like mountains shifting towards Moses, as told in the Old Testament, were believed to occur. As I have consistently argued, no theological research or argument has ever convinced me otherwise: if Moses were to resurrect today and attempt the same miracle, he would instead be required to move towards the mountain. This progression reflects how perspectives documented in the Old Testament differ from those in the New Testament.

The world is not static; change is constant, taking various forms–from climate change to the military might of nations asserting dominance over others. Time is of the essence, and the success of athletes is largely due to intensive training and substantial investments in acquiring the necessary equipment and facilities to enhance performance at global competitions. From this analysis, one can conclude that determination must be paired with serious effort; otherwise, it remains mere wishful thinking. While there is light at the end of the tunnel, the tunnel does not transform into the light of its own accord–one must possess the spiritual and physical resolve to push forward.

In Africa, our perception of time often hinders progress. For example, when someone is employed for a specific assignment, their punctuality and commitment frequently begin to wane after just three months on the job. Attendance becomes irregular, with excuses such as: 'The bus was late', 'Every available transport was full', or 'I had to delay my departure because my child began coughing, and I wanted to ensure the situation did not worsen before leaving.' Such attitudes reflect a cultural mindset that time is ours to manage as we see fit.

In contrast, many European countries take a stricter approach to time management. Persistent tardiness or frivolous excuses are tolerated only briefly. There, work environments often operate 24 hours a day, with shifts meticulously scheduled to ensure seamless operations. When one worker's shift ends, another is scheduled to take over, and the former often has personal commitments planned afterwards. A consistently late employee disrupts not only the workflow but also the schedules of others, leading to frustration and inefficiency. As a result, chronic lateness is seen as unprofessional and unproductive, frequently resulting in termination.

As the saying goes, 'The inventors of alarm clocks and mobile phone reminders are angels who keep us alert to the time.' People schedule their lives meticulously–from when to go to bed to when to leave home for appointments. Respecting these schedules ensures that tasks are completed efficiently and others are not inconvenienced. Time, after all, does not wait for anyone.

A businessman establishing a company must pursue various objectives, with the foremost being to generate profit and expand the business. This expansion may focus on its existing operations or diversify into other ventures identified as more profitable through thorough research. It is here that empirical research becomes indispensable, as no one invests time and money in initiatives unlikely to yield dividends.

For example, when applying to secure government contracts–such as constructing a flyover bridge, building new roads, or rehabilitating deteriorated ones–certain promises must be made. These include the timeline for project completion alongside cost quotations demonstrating the bidder's readiness to execute the work. Such factors enable the government to compare proposals from competing contractors and award the project based on merit. Authorities must be assured of the contractor's capacity, both technically and financially, to deliver the project successfully and in line with the architect's design, particularly after receiving an initial payment.

Equally vital is the need for transparency. The public must be informed about government projects, including the contractor's name, the cost, and the expected completion date for public use.

This is what constitutes open governance. Awarding contracts to cronies–whether relatives of governors or ministers–who fail to deliver, even after full payment, undermines trust and progress.

Similarly, people join societies or clubs for specific purposes. They are motivated by the benefits or experiences they expect to gain. Membership of an organisation often requires financial contributions or donations, as stipulated by its constitution. However, the objectives vary from one group to another. A social gathering focused on camaraderie differs significantly from a non-governmental organisation (NGO) whose aim may be to provide essential amenities to a particular community. Both may involve financial commitments, but their purposes are distinct. This is also unlike a professional organisation, where individuals join to network with like-minded peers and expand their knowledge. In such organisations, experienced professionals mentor recent graduates, facilitating growth and knowledge-sharing within the field.

One of Africa's persistent challenges, and a significant factor in its underdevelopment, is the lack of adventurousness. As the adage goes, 'Nothing ventured, nothing gained.' The assumption that divine intervention alone will solve all problems is a fallacy. Prayer is not an end in itself but a means to inspire action. Without sacrifice and relentless research, humanity would not have discovered electricity, invented motor vehicles, developed ships to cross oceans, or created aircraft to travel vast distances at unprecedented speeds.

A nation that depends solely on imports for nearly everything becomes a dependent state, unable to control its economic trajectory. Such a nation's circumstances are dictated by external forces from countries supplying its goods and services. The same God who created Europe also created Africa; however, God will not descend to manage the resources He endowed upon each region. As the saying goes, 'As you lay your bed, so you will lie on it.'

No nation can function effectively without laws governing it, nor can it thrive if such laws are poorly enforced or selectively applied. The law is the cornerstone of societal order, shaping behaviour and regulating daily activities. For instance, if business hours are legally set between 8 a.m. and 8 p.m., those violating this regulation must face the consequences. Failure to enforce such laws creates precedents that others will emulate, ultimately leading to chaos and lawlessness. In such conditions, a society becomes ungovernable, mired in disorder and instability.

CHAPTER SIXTEEN
THE AFRICAN VIRTUES

God is God. He created everything in heaven and on earth, including all people, irrespective of their religion, place of birth, or country of origin. Each region calls Him by a name in their languages, yet there is no language He does not understand, for He is the Lord of promises. He has declared that when we obey His commandments and follow His guidelines, He will hear our cries, accept us as His children, and grant our prayers and requests–so long as they do not bring us harm.

In Nigeria, the Hausa people, predominantly Muslim, call Him Allah. Devout Muslims pray five times daily, give alms to the poor, and fulfil the fifth pillar of Islam by undertaking the pilgrimage to Mecca and Medina, which is considered the final and most significant act of worship in Islam. However, God attaches conditions to His promises, and the pilgrimage is no exception. It is intended only for those who are in good health and possess the financial means to undertake it. Unfortunately, in Nigeria, these conditions have been misinterpreted by both Federal and State governments, who have distorted this divine principle. Rather than upholding the original purpose of the pilgrimage as a spiritual duty, the government has squandered national resources by transforming the Nigerian Pilgrimage Board–a welfare organisation–into an institution that sponsors individuals to perform this act of worship. This contravenes the principle of the fifth pillar of Islam and turns what should be a personal act of devotion into a tool of political manipulation. Politicians, eager to secure votes during elections, misuse public resources as charity to gain favour.

Among the Yoruba people, God is traditionally known as *Olúwa, Olórun,* or *Olódùmarè,* reflecting indigenous beliefs that predate external religious influences. Their ancestral worship includes numerous gods and deities, each with distinct roles and rituals. Notable among these are *Sàñgó, Oya, Obàtálá, Agemo, Òsun Òsogbo, Sòpònà, Òrìsà, Ifá, Ògún,* and others tied to natural elements such as water, fire, and iron. These beliefs, transmitted orally through generations, are often exploited by politicians during campaigns.

In contemporary Southwest Nigeria, politicians use cultural and religious beliefs as tools of persuasion during elections. To secure votes, candidates distribute gifts to impoverished individuals–a practice cynically referred to as *vote buying*. Items like five yards of Ankara fabric, ₦5000 in cash, half a bag of rice, or a packet of noodles are offered, often accompanied by coercive rituals. Voters might be made to swear oaths on sacred objects, taste blood, or cross over guns or cutlasses, binding them to a covenant of loyalty. Failure to fulfil this obligation is believed to invite severe consequences–death by car accident for breaking a cutlass covenant or death by gunshot for violating one made over a gun.

Politicians overlook the true purpose of governance, as 95% of them are not motivated by the well-being of the masses.

They neglect critical responsibilities such as protecting lives and property, fostering development, improving educational opportunities for children, providing free healthcare, reducing unemployment, and ensuring affordable food prices. Their primary focus lies in exploiting government resources for personal gain, benefiting themselves and their families.

They forget the wisdom once shared by President John F. Kennedy of the United States: 'Ask not what your country can do for you; ask what you can do for your country.' Sadly, such philosophy seems absent from our collective way of life.

The rate at which people are dying due to poverty is incalculable. Individuals who have served their fatherland for thirty-five years are not receiving their mandatory pension payments. Consequently, they cannot afford to consult a medical doctor for basic examinations, let alone be prescribed medication that might help them recover from minor and curable illnesses. This systemic failure underlines why Nigerian politicians seldom concede election losses. Those defeated often claim electoral fraud and proceed to court to reclaim their alleged mandate. Some of these cases linger in the courts for over three years without resolution.

According to the Nigerian Constitution, elections are held every four years for all political offices. The office of the President or Governor is limited to two terms of four years each, equating to a maximum of eight years. However, positions in the Senate, the House of Representatives, and the State Assembly are not similarly restricted. As long as a representative's constituency continues to be re-elected, they can retain their position indefinitely.

There was a time when honesty and dedication to duty defined traditional practices, including the work of herbalists–*Babalawos*. These herbalists conducted consultations on behalf of their clients, performing rituals and sacrifices such as offering goats, dogs, chickens, or blood donations. These sacrifices often yielded the desired results, usually within seven days. Herbalists in those days maintained a certain mystique; they were neither commonly seen in public nor mingling openly like ordinary individuals. Instead, they commanded fear, respect, and reverence. Encounters with herbalists are typically rare and reserved for moments of serious crises, requiring consultation for solutions.

Upon arriving at their enclave, visitors are expected to adhere to specific protocols of greeting and respect. The standard greeting, *Aboruboye o*–meaning 'I wish you success in your endeavours'–was met with the response, 'Ifa agbe o', signifying a blessing from the Ifa deity and assurance that the visitor's problem had been addressed or a path forward had opened. The herbalist would then consult the oracle, casting Ifa to define the root of the problem and offer a solution based on the oracle's message.

Herbalists played pivotal roles in traditional matters, including the selection of kings or *Otunbas* for royal positions. When a royal stool became vacant due to the passing of the occupant, the competition to succeed them often became intense. Those who believed they were qualified to ascend to the position of king or *Otunba* would spend heavily to boost their status. However, the final decision rested with the Ifa oracle. The kingmakers, acting as the custodians of tradition, would compile a list of candidates, and consult the Ifa oracle. Once the Ifa identifies the chosen candidate, all others would gracefully step aside and support the designated individual.

Regrettably, much of this tradition has been eroded by politics. Politicians have infiltrated and corrupted the processes that once safeguarded the sanctity of our traditions and customs. As a result, our time-honoured practices have been dismantled, and the influence of modern politics continues to overshadow the rich cultural heritage that once guided every step of our lives.

It is the politicians, particularly the governors, who give the final approval for rulership in every town under their governance, selecting whomever they choose. How can one expect to command respect in a township where they are not the people's choice to rule?

In the eastern part of the country, the use of political influence in selecting traditional rulers mirrors what we are now experiencing in Yorubaland. The selection of an *Obi*–the head of a town–and the local chief, often appointed to oversee an age group, is typically determined by the *Obi*. My colleague in journalism, Babatunde Kolade Otitoju, was recently honoured with a chieftaincy title in one of the eastern states. This recognition was based on his historical knowledge, consistent honesty, and open-minded contributions during debates on national issues at the *Journalist Hangout*.

The fact that someone from Kogi State was awarded one of the region's most prestigious chieftaincy titles is remarkable. It underscores Nigeria's potential as a unified entity. Notably, Otitoju did not purchase the title nor contribute philanthropically to the region that honoured him. This recognition was purely merit-based.

Historically, political interventions have often influenced the selection of *Obis* and local chiefs, with little or no reference to traditional oracles in conferring chieftaincy titles. The eastern region is renowned for its Christian allegiance, particularly to the Catholic Church. However, religion holds no power over the selection of traditional rulers. Those who are selected often attend church services to thank God and express generosity, but the church itself has no direct influence on the process.

The eastern region was the first in Nigeria to embrace Christianity, introduced by colonial missionaries. Consequently, Catholic doctrines are deeply rooted in its communities.

The focus of this chapter shifts to religion in Yorubaland. As a tribe, why did we betray the God who bestowed upon us our indigenous form of worship? For reasons difficult to justify, we turned away from our own God–a mighty God–under the influence of Muslim preachers from Saudi Arabia and Christian missionaries from Europe. Yorubas once held deep and honest reverence for their deities, whose responses to their petitions were swift, often with visible signs like thunder from the heavens.

OBASHIP IN YORUBALAND

The moment you are crowned an *Oba* of a town, you are bound by specific codes of conduct. You must avoid disrespectful settings, refrain from granting press interviews without valid reasons, and adhere strictly to the expected decorum, including appropriate attire. You are seen as the father of all traditional and secular religions. As such, you are obligated to attend all religious ceremonies and maintain a position of neutrality, giving equal respect to all faiths.

For instance, the Ooni of Ife exemplifies this ideal by participating in various religious events without prejudice. An *Oba* is also expected to be impartial in political matters, providing guidance and blessings to all. This is the hallmark of a true custodian of culture, religion, and governance.

In contrast, the Oluwo of Iwo recently caused controversy by marrying a Fulani woman from Kano, a member of another royal family. Speculations were rife about his motives, with critics suggesting he sought recognition in Saudi Arabia and potential financial benefits. However, many refrained from making open accusations. In one public statement, the Oluwo declared that he would never permit the practice of traditional religion in his domain, a position that sparked criticism. One commentator noted that his selection as *Oba* did not follow the conventional traditional process. Another claimed, with authority, that his appointment was solely the result of the Osun State governor's decision.

In Yorubaland, the process of replacing a ruler who has passed away involves strict traditions. Kingmakers review the history and qualifications of candidates, ensuring they come from the royal lineage. In the past, individuals related to the royal family through the maternal line were deemed ineligible to ascend the throne. However, this tradition was broken during the reign of the late Ooni of Ife, Oba Okunade Sijuwade, who was deemed eligible because his mother was of royal lineage in Ile-Ife.

CHAPTER SEVENTEEN

TIME FLIES

Every step in life is marked by its own time. Imagine you wish to travel from one country to another. Once upon a time, sea voyages by ship were commonplace, but today, such journeys have largely become obsolete. They are now mostly embraced by elderly individuals who aspire to explore the world aboard specially designed ships. These modern vessels are equipped with every facility imaginable to make passengers feel as though they are in the comfort of their homes during extended tours, which can last for six months or more.

The ship stops at designated ports, as outlined in the company's prospectus–an essential document that travellers must thoroughly read and agree to before committing to the journey by way of a signed contract. Historical records preserved in archives remind us that travelling by ship from Lagos, Nigeria, to the United Kingdom once took approximately two to three weeks. However, as technology advanced and innovations were applied to sea travel, the duration gradually reduced to two weeks. This shift was partly due to increased efficiency in handling passengers and goods, enabling more direct journeys between Lagos and London. The need to halt at multiple harbours along the

West African coastline was eliminated, significantly expediting the voyage.

Though time-consuming compared to today's standards, these sea journeys were remarkably convenient, particularly for large families. They were designed to be as stress-free as possible, with ample provisions ensuring travellers enjoyed a level of comfort akin to being at home. Food, drinks, and recreational facilities were abundant. Gymnasiums offered physical exercise opportunities, while ship corridors provided space for leisurely walks. Passengers could relax in dedicated recreational areas, ensuring their comfort throughout the voyage.

Despite such comforts, travelling from Lagos, for instance, often meant not seeing one's family for at least two weeks. This extended separation sometimes led to significant anxiety for relatives eagerly anticipating the travellers' arrival at their destination. The anxiety often stemmed from fears of potential mishaps–an all-too-common concern at the time. We have read accounts of ships running aground during sea storms or their funnels striking underwater rocks, events that could result in minor injuries or, in some cases, more serious accidents for passengers on board. Such dangers only heightened the apprehension of those awaiting their loved ones' safe return.

Yet, despite the risks, sea voyages remain etched in history as a crucial part of global exploration and connection–a reminder that every great journey requires time, trust, and a spirit of adventure.

The era of travelling for many days or weeks by ship gradually faded into history as air travel became dominant, facilitated by modern technology. Although the cost of purchasing flight tickets increased significantly, the anxiety and isolation caused by prolonged separations from family were almost eliminated.

What was once a two- or three-week journey by sea was replaced by a mere six-hour flight from Lagos to London. However, with the advent of air travel came an increased fear of accidents, as flights are statistically perceived as more prone to mishaps than sea voyages. Yet, as circumstances evolve, so too do people's desires and expectations. It is now commonplace to bid farewell to loved ones in Lagos in the morning and greet awaiting relations at London Airport in the evening–or to meet those hosting you at their homes by the following morning.

One significant adjustment necessitated by air travel is the limitation on luggage size. Whereas ships could accommodate substantial amounts of cargo presented at the harbour, aeroplanes operate under far stricter weight and size constraints. Travellers must, therefore, accept a measure of sacrifice to enjoy the speed and convenience modern air travel provides.

Technology has further revolutionised travel by introducing online trading, purchasing, and booking systems. Travellers can now buy flight tickets at their convenience and choose their preferred departure and arrival dates. Airlines operate diverse schedules, with some flights departing in the morning and others at night, depending on the allocations granted by the host country's Airport Authority. For instance, when examining flight routes between London and Lagos, direct flights are operating between the two cities. Conversely, some airlines split the journey into two legs, stopping first in their home countries–Amsterdam, France, Qatar, or Morocco–before proceeding to the final destination, such as Lagos, Accra, or Johannesburg. This system allows airlines to consolidate passengers from multiple origins heading to shared destinations.

Additionally, technology has made the process of booking flights both simple and accessible. Flights can now be reserved months in advance, often at significantly lower prices. This is particularly advantageous during high-demand periods, such as school holidays or summer seasons. It affords travellers the flexibility to adjust their itineraries should unexpected changes arise in their circumstances.

CHAPTER EIGHTEEN

THE WORLD OF TOMORROW

The first question that comes to mind when confronted with a topic such as the one displayed above is this: what is tomorrow? Tomorrow, as defined by the natural order of creation, is the day that follows today. As today concludes at midnight–when most people are either asleep or at home watching their favourite television programmes–few, if any, can definitively say they witnessed the exact moment when one day transitions into the next. Unless one has a specific reason to monitor the passing time, whether by watching a wall clock, a wristwatch, or the clock on a mobile phone, the shift often goes unnoticed. Exceptions occur when the change is marked by significant events, such as the birth of a child, the passing of a loved one (as sadly happened to many during the COVID-19 pandemic), or a traumatic experience that leaves a lasting imprint on one's memory.

For those who devote their lives to monitoring time, preserving history, or researching planetary or weather changes–a small but crucial segment of the world's population–such moments hold profound significance. These individuals understand that our actions, or lack thereof, today bear a lasting impact on tomorrow. Recognising the irrevocability of the past, they emphasise the need to prepare for the future. Tomorrow, after all, represents the future–a fresh opportunity to strive for what is yet to be achieved, to amend the mistakes of yesterday, and to pursue greater aspirations.

As beings created in the image of God, we are endowed with the ability to distinguish between right and wrong. This sense of moral responsibility enables us to experience remorse for our misdeeds, to apologise to those we have wronged, and to seek forgiveness from God. Such acts of reflection and repentance are uniquely human, setting us apart from other creatures. Through genuine contrition, we acknowledge our errors–be they unintentional or otherwise–and commit to not repeating them. This process is central to personal growth and spiritual alignment, as illustrated in the Scriptures.

Consider the contrast between Amaziah, as recounted in the Book of 2 Chronicles, and King David. Amaziah, who ascended to the throne at the age of twenty-five and reigned for twenty-nine years, outwardly obeyed God. Yet, his heart was not truly with the Lord. In contrast, King David, despite his numerous sins, served God wholeheartedly. This distinction underscores the importance of sincerity and the condition of one's heart in the pursuit of righteousness.

Viewing tomorrow as a day that might not come to fruition necessitates preparation for all eventualities. Countless people retire to bed with carefully crafted plans for the following day, only to never awaken. Others face unexpected emergencies, finding themselves rushed to hospital and placed on life support, caught between life and death. In my youth, such a state was aptly described as 'one foot on earth and one foot in heaven'– a precarious transition where the outcome is uncertain.

In the developed world, tomorrow is often envisioned as an arena for exploration and advancement, whether in science, technology, or other frontiers of human endeavour. Such ventures are sometimes viewed with scepticism by individuals in underdeveloped regions, who dismiss them as madness or acts of lunacy. For instance, space exploration–travelling to the moon– may seem unimaginable to those whose understanding is shaped by traditional religious teachings, which often define existence as being confined to heaven and earth. These perspectives highlight the vast differences in how various societies perceive and prepare for tomorrow, revealing the richness and complexity of our shared human experience.

Science and technology, extensively researched and developed through continuous human effort, have revealed to us the vastness of the heavens and the earth. Our planet, Earth, is one among many, yet it is uniquely home to human beings and animals. Other planets, in contrast, may not be inhabited as ours is. Some may have harboured life centuries or millennia ago. This reality underscores the importance of planning for tomorrow, even though we cannot control its outcomes. As the wise proverb goes, 'Nothing ventured, nothing gained.' Religious teachings assure us that tomorrow will be better than today, but does such progress happen automatically?

The passage of time–from seconds to minutes, hours to days, weeks to months, and even years–shapes our perspectives on life. These measures of time were named and organised by humanity, not divinely decreed. While both the Bible and the Holy Quran urge us to obey the commandments of God (or Allah) and His will, they also make clear that faith without effort will not provide for our needs–unless, perhaps, we are professional beggars, which is not the purpose for which God designed us. To make a meaningful impact and leave behind a lasting legacy, one must engage in research, experimentation, and industrious work.

Consider a farmer. Only through sowing crops can he expect a bountiful harvest. If he remains idle at home, he should not delude himself into thinking that an untended farm will yield food for his family. Such an expectation is sheer fantasy, akin to building castles in the air. Even during the era of the Soviet Union, when the state proclaimed equality for all and a fair distribution of resources, disparities were evident. Some individuals lived and prospered better than the common folk. Within the hierarchy of the workforce, those with higher education, such as university degrees, could not be equated–financially or professionally–with unskilled workers.

The reward for hard work is a better standard of living, often tied to profit and productivity. Conversely, the outcome of laziness is subsistence living, barely getting by. Nowhere in the world are all citizens truly equal; such claims are little more than political rhetoric, crafted to make the disadvantaged feel included and to instil a sense of shared rights among people from vastly different walks of life.

CHAPTER NINETEEN

LIVING WITH ARTIFICIAL INTELLIGENCE AND ROBOT

ARTIFICIAL INTELLIGENCE:

The modern world is experiencing a way of life that, a decade ago, might have seemed like pure fiction. Every day, someone is exploring and inventing advancements in modern technology designed to simplify life, making it easier than the experiences of previous generations. These developments can be considered an expanded realisation of what was once imagined as *the world of tomorrow.*

Artificial Intelligence, or AI as it will henceforth be referred to, has permeated numerous aspects of daily life, significantly transforming traditional methods of conducting tasks. AI has been defined as a technological approach that facilitates functions such as generating, classifying, and performing tasks like image analysis and speech recognition. It represents the ability of machines to replicate cognitive functions typically associated with the human mind, including perceiving, reasoning, and learning. By reducing friction and improving analytical efficiency across organisations, AI has led to notable cost reductions and enhanced resource utilisation. Its development is primarily driven by the desire for more efficient task performance, replacing what would otherwise be done manually.

AI also connects users globally, enabling businesses to identify and prioritise their most valuable customers. As a general-purpose technology, its applications extend across industries and academia, analogous to the role of electricity or computers. For instance, in language translation, modern mobile phones can instantly interpret phrases spoken in one language into another, providing translations within seconds. AI-powered image recognition systems are invaluable in criminal justice, ensuring accuracy during police identification parades. Similarly, AI optimises decision-making, reduces time wastage, and increases profitability, as seen in credit scoring, where it expedites loan decisions for personal or business purposes, such as e-commerce ventures.

In agriculture, AI enhances productivity by identifying areas needing irrigation, fertilisation, or pesticide treatment. It also aids agronomists in research and development, such as predicting crop ripening times. For example, farmers can monitor soil moisture levels or use autonomous tractors that continue ploughing without a driver, operated remotely. On some televised programmes, we see unmanned harvesting equipment monitored by farmers from the comfort of their homes. AI has revolutionised poultry farming too, with mechanised systems dispensing feed automatically, a testament to its influence on modern agricultural methodologies.

In the United Kingdom, Artificial Intelligence is being used by the NHS to support clinical decision-making, analyse scans and test results, and manage appointment scheduling. Dr Malte Gerhold of the Health Foundation Charity observed that public involvement is crucial for the government to achieve its ambition of digitising the NHS. While there is some hesitancy regarding AI-powered tools, such as robots assisting with personal care like washing and dressing, a significant proportion of individuals support sharing their data to further AI development in the NHS. Dr Gerhold stated that when appropriately implemented, AI has the potential to relieve staff of administrative and clinical burdens.

Innovations such as temporary liquid ink tattoos for the scalp are also making headlines. These tattoos help doctors measure brain activity without requiring patients to shave their heads. The liquid flows through the hair onto the scalp, and once it dries, it functions as a sensor, detecting brain activity. This technology presents a less cumbersome alternative to the traditional practice of marking electrodes on patients' scalps, which involved pencils, rulers, adhesive electrodes, and cumbersome wiring to computers–a process that used to take hours to complete.

ROBOT:

A robot is a jointed machine designed to replicate the functions of a human being, particularly because it is programmable by a computer, enabling it to perform complex tasks automatically. A robot can be guided by an external control device, or its controls may be embedded within its system. Consequently, new advancements define a robot as any automatically operated machine that replaces human effort, even if it does not physically resemble a human being. Despite this, robots often perform tasks like humans. By extension, robotics is the engineering discipline concerned with the design, construction, and operation of robots.

The modern term *robot* originates from the Czech word for *forced labour*, highlighting the mechanical labour origins of the concept. Robots have been invented to undertake tasks that would otherwise involve significant human effort, such as relieving you of weekend chores like wrestling with a cumbersome vacuum cleaner, dealing with dust, or tending to an overgrown garden. These machines are reliable, never complain, and do not take days off. They execute their tasks seamlessly, one step at a time, with the ability to shift from one assignment to another when programmed to do so. Customisable cleaning robots, for instance, can refill their water tanks and empty their onboard dustbins autonomously.

Robotic gadgets are continually evolving with innovations that enhance functionality. For example, long-lasting batteries are now common, enabling multiple operations throughout the day. When their power drops to a certain level, these robots automatically return to their charging stations.

Recently, I came across a Facebook video showcasing a robot being used as a labourer to carry five bags of cement on its shoulders. It moved the cement from a truck to a designated area at a construction site–a task that would have required five humans or one individual making five trips to complete.

There are many types of robots, each designed to perform specific functions, both within homes and outdoor spaces.

1. **Segway Navimow H500E:** This automated lawn mower delivers impressive results, largely because of its ability to navigate gardens accurately and efficiently. For more intricate gardens, an optional VisionFence camera with advanced AI obstacle avoidance ensures precision. The machine's rugged construction pairs well with large tread wheels that glide effortlessly over mud and rough terrain.
2. **EcoVacs Winbot W2:** A revolutionary window-cleaning assistant, this device puts your least favourite chore on autopilot. It combines exceptional suction technology with dual cleaning solutions, enabling it to clean vertical and horizontal surfaces effectively. One standout feature is its smart navigation system, which maps window surfaces and ensures no spots are missed. For added reliability, a backup battery prevents power outages from causing unexpected falls. Its washable and reusable cleaning pads contribute to more sustainable cleaning routines.

The robotics industry is highly competitive, with manufacturers constantly showcasing their latest inventions through advertisements and distribution channels to raise public awareness. Paper brochures, telephone marketing, and digital advertisements play a significant role in promoting these products to potential users. Moreover, modern televised activities are frequently sponsored by companies eager to highlight their technological advancements, introducing innovations to a wider audience.

CHAPTER TWENTY

TRAVELLING IN THE MODERN WORLD

In one of the previous chapters, I mentioned the use of clocks or mobile alarm systems to help individuals wake up and start their daily assignments, whether going to work, attending a conference, or engaging in business activities such as running a shop or a transport system. In this chapter, I aim to compare the systems commonly used in Nigeria with those prevalent in developed countries. I intend to remind political leaders of the advancements they have experienced or witnessed during their travels as students, visitors, or on medical vacations, yet have failed to implement for the benefit of their citizens to ensure a modern standard of living.

What I will highlight is not unfamiliar to them, as they have either seen or benefited from such systems while abroad, particularly when visiting their children who are enrolled in higher education institutions in these advanced countries. It is crucial to examine the means of travelling within towns and cities in other countries to understand how our political leaders have failed to provide significant infrastructure improvements that could enhance the quality of life in Nigeria.

I frequently observe ministers and governors moving in motorcades consisting of six or seven vehicles, accompanied by officials and security personnel from the Police, DSS, and local security agencies. These motorcades, marked by blaring sirens, compel other road users to park by the roadside, signalling the imminent passage of a so-called *very important person.* It is worth recalling that these leaders attained their positions through our votes, cast during elections in which they made grand promises to improve citizens' lives and safeguard their properties. Despite their commitments to address insecurity, road hazards, potholes, and illegal toll collections at garages, their performance during their tenure often leaves much to be desired. The state of affairs is better left for the populace to assess and draw their conclusions.

On a brighter note, the Lagos State Government has introduced a commendable transportation system: the Blue Line rail service, and more recently, the Red Line. These modern train systems connect major parts of the state, facilitating prompt and comfortable commutes for workers. Such an initiative is unprecedented on the African continent. While it does not function as an intercity railway connecting various regions of the country, its focus on intra-state transportation represents significant progress. Notably, a similar plan was envisaged and initiated by the late Lateef Jakande, who reportedly secured funding and awarded contracts to commence the project. Unfortunately, the plan was scrapped by the military regime of General Buhari and Tunde Idiagbon following their overthrow of President Shagari's government in 1985.

The intra-state train service in Lagos is a commendable achievement, provided it does not face the challenges plaguing other parts of the country's rail system, such as vandalism. In certain areas, rail tracks have been stolen and sold to buyers in neighbouring countries. Is this a case of greed, wickedness, or sheer poverty driving individuals to destroy national assets? Or are there unseen forces orchestrating these acts, using others to undermine the nation's infrastructure? Such actions raise pressing questions about our national pride and collective responsibility in developing the country.

During the 1940s and 1950s, owning a bicycle was a significant symbol of pride. Our fathers used bicycles not only for leisure rides around town but also for travelling to their villages to farm. They would ride out in the morning and return to town in the evening. The most admired bicycles were those with chrome finishes, and men riding them in cultural attire (often white Buba and Sokoto) were greeted with respect–a bow of the head or a wave of the hand. Women often curtsied in acknowledgement.

In another book, I referenced a young man named Mushafau, a one-legged individual who worked as a bicycle repairer and rental operator. Mushafau's enterprise played a pivotal role in teaching many of us to ride bicycles during our youth. His story serves as a reminder of the resilience and ingenuity that once defined our communities and highlights the stark contrast with the underdeveloped infrastructure and systemic failures we face today.

As extensively noted, modern technology has become an integral part of our lives. In the United Kingdom, a country favoured by our leaders for the education of their children, members of the upper echelons of society frequently travel to visit their wards. These visits often coincide with organised conferences, the signing of contracts on behalf of their states, vocational holidays, or simply family visits. It raises the question: during their time in the UK, do they not observe the infrastructural advancements that contribute to making life more pleasant and comfortable for citizens? Instead, it seems that many neglect to apply such observations to improving the political and social environments of their home country. This indicates a lack of commitment to creating a meaningful political impact.

In the UK, it is common for families to aspire to buy bicycles for their children, even from the age of one, beginning with toy models designed to teach balance and coordination. The bicycles are regularly upgraded every two years to suit the growing child. Morning streets are a lively scene of toddlers riding two-wheel tricycles, seated at the front or back of their parents' bikes. This is facilitated by well-maintained and safe pavements, courtesy of government-provided infrastructure. These designated paths allow children to play and exercise safely outdoors.

Bicycle sellers in the UK often have trade-in schemes where old bicycles can be exchanged for newer models at discounted prices. Families who cannot afford new bikes may opt for second-hand options, which remain functional and reliable. The maxim, 'cut your coat according to your cloth', aptly applies here.

The City of London, in particular, has championed cycling by creating exclusive lanes for cyclists. These lanes protect them from reckless drivers, especially truck drivers, who often fail to check their blind spots. This innovation has encouraged more people to adopt cycling for commuting or exercise, transforming the way residents navigate the city during the busy *rush hours*. Additionally, major companies, including prominent banks, sponsor public bicycle schemes by branding bicycles with their names and logos. These bicycles are strategically stationed near train and underground stations or at major road junctions. With the use of Artificial Intelligence (AI), the rental and payment processes are streamlined: users simply touch a designated area with their debit card to unlock the bicycle, use it as needed, and pay for the duration upon its return to the station.

The efficiency and foresight of such programmes are truly remarkable, particularly when observed in public spaces where young children confidently ride tricycles on tarred or concreted paths. This often prompts the question: when will Nigeria develop similar infrastructure? Open spaces with proper flooring for children to play near their homes after school are sorely needed. Unfortunately, many lands earmarked for public use are sold by local, state, or federal officials to private developers for residential housing. Does this mean that laws governing land boundaries are ineffective in Nigeria? The culpability of the Ministry of Lands and Works in this matter cannot be overstated.

As one journalist remarked, Nigeria's stagnation is largely attributable to the greed of government officials, extending even to civil servants. After 64 years of independence, the phrase 'Nigeria will be great' has become a hollow mockery. Those in power live lives of luxury, disconnected from the struggles of the citizens. Meanwhile, many ordinary Nigerians resort to corruption or exploitation to secure their future. A newspaper once reported that truck drivers transporting goods between Kano and Calabar were compelled to pay bribes totalling ₦600,000 per trip at police and military checkpoints. Delays caused by refusing such demands often result in perishable goods being spoiled or stolen, exacerbating the challenges of doing business in the country.

Yet, all is not bleak for Nigeria. Recently, the nation celebrated a major achievement when Chidimma Adetshina became the first Nigerian to win the position of first runner-up at the Miss Universe 2024 contest in Mexico. Chidimma's story is one of resilience. Born in Soweto, South Africa, to a Nigerian father and a Mozambican mother, she faced rejection by the South African government, which classified her mother as an illegal resident. Despite being raised and educated in South Africa, she embraced her Nigerian heritage, representing Taraba State in the Miss Nigeria Universe competition. Her victory there earned her the opportunity to represent Nigeria on the global stage.

Abike Dabiri-Erewa, Chairperson of the Nigerians in Diaspora Commission, lauded Chidimma's determination and focus. Her success exemplifies the potential for greatness that resides within the nation's citizens–a glimmer of hope in an otherwise challenging national narrative.

The competition, described as one of the most thrilling in recent years, celebrated the talents, intelligence, and elegance of women from around the globe. Meanwhile, South Africa is currently investigating claims that Chidimma's mother assumed the identity of a South African woman. Chidimma has brought Nigeria immense pride, achieving a recognition no other African country has attained.

An election was concluded in the United States of America a few weeks ago, in November 2024. The results highlighted the unsavoury nature of politics–a game that demands ruggedness, desperation, obstinacy, and an intense craving for personal recognition. Those who enter the political arena often do so with the hope of securing fame and global attention should they succeed. However, the contest proves time and again that education is not the ultimate determinant of electoral success.

Education may help a candidate craft practicable and implementable policies based on advice from supporters and campaign aides. It could also guide them on what to say during political rallies, appealing to public interest. Yet, such strategies do not always resonate with the majority. After all, elections are won by numbers, and majority votes decide the race.

If education were the primary criterion for electing leaders, Kamala Harris, the Democratic Party candidate, would likely have won. However, she was up against a rival known for his extreme desperation and a figurative *wardrobe* packed with skeletons. This illustrates the paradox of democracy in even the most developed nations: the electorate's choices are shaped more by perception than by education or morality.

Interestingly, there were no allegations of vote manipulation, ballot snatching, or vote-buying in this U.S. election. No defeated candidate threatened legal action to contest the results. The process ran its course without the hallmarks of controversy that plague elections in some other parts of the world.

In contrast, consider the recent governorship election in Ondo, Nigeria. A young man, driving a modest car, was stopped by the police–likely acting on a tip-off. Inside the car boot were *Ghana Must Go* bags heavily loaded with undisclosed contents. However, the bags were not opened publicly for transparency.

Later reports claimed they contained money intended for vote buying.

This raises pertinent questions. Who owned the car and the money? Who gave the money to the driver, and who was supposed to receive it? How much money was inside the bags? Such ambiguities exemplify Nigeria's tendency to leap to conclusions and disseminate unverified information. These lapses erode public trust in the electoral process.

Nigeria still has a long way to go–perhaps ten more critical steps–before we achieve electoral maturity.

CHAPTER TWENTY-ONE

WHEN RETIRED FROM WORK

During the medieval period in Europe, before the Industrial Revolution, children as young as seven were compelled to work in factories manufacturing goods for export. They endured gruelling shifts lasting 12 to 15 hours a day, six days a week. This wasn't for their personal needs or indulgences, as drug misuse–so prevalent today–was not a societal issue at the time. I recall the story of the renowned missionary, Mary Slessor[3], who began working in a textile factory at the age of 11, using her wages to support her family. It was during this time that she read about the pagan rituals and sacrifices occurring in Calabar, Nigeria in the 19th century. Driven by a sense of purpose, she left her job and responded to the call of the gospel, dedicating over forty years of her life as a missionary in Calabar.

There is, indeed, a time for everything. What one aspires to achieve at 20 is often unattainable at 50. Human bodies have limits, and as we age, these limits become evident. From the age

---

3 Bastian, M. L. (2001). " The demon superstition": Abominable twins and mission culture in Onitsha history. *Ethnology*, 13-27.

of 40 onwards, physical decline may necessitate the use of walking aids for some. This highlights the importance of easing into life's later stages, as even a minor accident can lead to permanent physical damage. To remain active in today's tech-driven workforce, individuals must plan their lives carefully. Otherwise, age will take the reins. Exceptions exist, such as in the United States, where I once saw an 89-year-old man honoured at a retirement ceremony. His sustained health and consistent performance were remarkable, allowing his employer to overlook his age.

In the United Kingdom, most office jobs are contract-based, and renewals depend on several factors. The first is conduct: how you interact with colleagues is reflected in annual or periodic assessments, including punctuality and attendance. The second is productivity–punctuality is famously the soul of business, and delays can hinder the workflow of others reliant on timely contributions. Thirdly, adaptability to modern working methods is critical. With information technology evolving unprecedentedly, regular training helps workers stay abreast of new methodologies. Finally, age can play a significant role in contract renewal. At a certain point in life or after serving a specified number of years, employees must consider alternative plans for their future.

As some writers have wisely noted: if you do not leave the job, the job will eventually leave you. At a certain age, people find themselves unable to perform tasks they managed effortlessly two decades earlier. Physical agility wanes and cognitive sharpness diminishes. Additionally, younger, highly educated individuals entering the workforce must be allowed to apply their acquired skills, necessitating an environment where they can thrive.

In Nigeria, civil service rules stipulate that employees must retire voluntarily upon reaching the age of 60 or after 45 years of service, whichever comes first. The policy, however, is silent on retrenchment processes, which often lack standardisation. While the Labour Law endorses a *first in, first out* principle, this is more of a theoretical framework than a practical one. Courts are granted authority over retrenchment cases at Labour Tribunals, but employers frequently intimidate workers by claiming such cases fall outside judicial jurisdiction. Retrenched employees are deemed surplus to requirements, often as a result of organisational restructuring, and their dismissal is treated as inevitable.

In developed countries, particularly the United Kingdom, before retrenching a worker who has served for over two years, employers are required to ensure their benefits are packaged and promptly handed to them. The practice of perpetually telling an employee 'Come today, come tomorrow' constitutes a serious breach of labour law, and the penalties for such violations are severe.

Additionally, the government supports individuals below pension age by providing weekly stipends, often referred to by names such as Jobseeker's Allowance. This enables unemployed individuals to maintain a basic standard of living. Further financial assistance is made available for those with families to care for. When a Nigerian company or government parastatal with branches in the UK folds up or becomes liquidated, its UK-based staff must be paid their full entitlements without delay. Failure to comply may result in the Nigerian government being taken to the Labour Court or tribunal. Such scenarios would attract widespread negative publicity across newspapers and result in heavy fines for non-compliance with the host country's laws and regulations.

In most developed countries, there is indeed life after retirement. Retirement opens a new chapter for the working class in Europe and the United States of America. Pensioners enjoy privileges that grant them access to certain public services. For instance, disabled individuals in London are entitled to free transport on public buses, trains, and the underground after 9 a.m. until the close of service. Pensioners can also join various clubs that offer rebates on activities, fostering community interaction and engagement.

Pensions are usually paid directly into bank accounts at the end of each month. However, for those preferring weekly payments, arrangements can be made for cash to be collected at the nearest post office upon presentation of a government-issued letter. Many recreation centres for pensioners are furnished like luxurious establishments. These centres, which often resemble five-star hotels, provide spaces for social interaction. Drinks, including tea, coffee, snacks, and soft beverages, are sold at discounted rates. When visiting these venues, one might easily mistake the attendees for guests at a wedding–well-dressed, neat, smart, and wearing broad smiles. These special facilities operate from 9 a.m. until 11 p.m., symbolising the vibrancy of post-retirement life.

To promote health, the government advises retirees to engage in daily activities like morning runs, cycling, and gym sessions in the evening. Although gyms are not directly funded by the government, discounted rates are often available for pensioners in facilities that use government-provided buildings. Those living in council houses benefit from rent discounts, and their council taxes are significantly reduced. Public buses in London are equipped to accommodate individuals in wheelchairs. Bus drivers ensure ease of boarding by lowering a platform to bridge the kerb and the bus. The entire process is monitored by the driver to guarantee passenger's safety, showcasing a combination of advanced technology and care for the vulnerable.

For elderly or disabled individuals requiring assistance, the government provides various housing and care options. Some choose to remain in their homes, where care companies send staff to assist them once, twice, or even three times a day, depending on their needs. These services are funded by the council or borough. Others are relocated to government-managed care homes, where meals may be communal or individually prepared by residents with the ability and inclination. Managers oversee the welfare of residents, including security and laundry services, ensuring a dignified living experience.

Respect, in these societies, is a fundamental cultural principle. For instance, able-bodied individuals give priority to the elderly and disabled on public transport. At bus stops and train stations, they step aside to allow the less mobile to board or disembark first. There is no need to rush or show impatience, as another train or bus will usually arrive within minutes. This culture of gentleness and humility is not imposed but stems from an ingrained sense of duty to care for others.

Even those classified as rough sleepers or homeless–individuals without a place to call home–are not neglected. Councils, churches, and supermarkets often collaborate to provide food banks, ensuring no one is entirely overlooked. Homeless individuals are guaranteed basic sustenance, including hot tea, snacks, or bread in the morning and cooked meals in the afternoon.

This is the essence of what is referred to as a **welfare state**.

CHAPTER TWENTY-TWO
THE FUTURE AS IT SHOULD BE

Perhaps the stagnation of Nigeria, from one generation to the next, stems from the failure of our fathers or political leaders to leave behind a meaningful legacy when abdicating their positions. Despite over 64 years of independence, one cannot help but observe that wherever one turns, there is little novelty, admiration, or significance to rival what exists in developed countries. While towns are expanding, the corresponding infrastructural development to ensure sustainable growth and reflect proper planning seems conspicuously absent.

For example, baby pushchairs–an essential item to ensure children's comfort when accompanying their parents–highlight a lack of prioritised modernisation. These pushchairs provide security and convenience, with children seated comfortably and fastened securely to prevent falls or the risk of being taken by unscrupulous individuals. Working-class mothers in particular benefit from the availability of various designs, sizes, and prices offered by specialist shops. However, for those facing financial challenges, such as single mothers or divorced women whose partners neglect their responsibilities, the government often intervenes to assist with such essentials, supporting them in the arduous task of raising children.

Every morning, I am fascinated by the sight of mothers taking their three-year-old children to school. Typically, the mother walks on the roadside while the child, regardless of gender, leads or trails behind, riding a tricycle. One of the earliest lessons taught in schools involves road safety. Children are instructed to locate traffic lights, approach them cautiously, and wait for the green light, accompanied by a sound signal–a helpful feature for those with hearing or vision impairments. Many modern traffic lights now include countdown timers, ensuring safe crossing as the clock ticks from 10 to 0. Parents are often seen carrying their children's tricycles as they return home after the morning drop-off, and later when heading back to collect their wards.

Witnessing children's morning routines in the UK feels like watching a scene from a lively film. Their buoyant attitudes, playful energy, and the endearing ways they hold their parents' hands or chase one another along pavements are delightful. The scene becomes even more heartwarming when siblings, whether brothers or brother and sister, interact, or when schoolmates cross paths. The cheerful smiles, hugs, and warm greetings defy adequate description. A contributing factor to this jubilant atmosphere is undoubtedly the environment, which seems designed to nurture such joy.

Both children and adults in the UK have also embraced skateboarding as a mode of transport and recreation. Skateboarding, whether used to commute to school or work, adds a unique vibrancy to public spaces. However, the way some young people manoeuvre skateboards–often on roads or pavements–can be nerve-wracking. It is particularly alarming when they simultaneously engage with their phones or wear headphones that impair their spatial awareness, risking collisions with vehicles or pedestrians. Watching them fills me with a mixture of admiration and apprehension, as I silently pray for their safety.

Skateboarding, as a sport, has also evolved to include thrilling stunts, such as navigating artificial ramps and executing dramatic jumps. Though the risk of injury is ever-present, participants appear undeterred. The widespread availability of mobile phones ensures that in the event of an accident, help can be summoned quickly, whether from an ambulance or the police. This blending of sport and practicality has turned skateboarding into a universal, and often exhilarating, form of activity that epitomises the adventurous spirit of modern youth.

In the United Kingdom, ambulances are required to arrive at the scene of an accident within ten minutes. Failure to meet this timeframe can lead to fatalities, and the NHS Trust responsible for the area may be taken to court. In such cases, a mere apology is insufficient; instead, the organisation could face substantial fines or sanctions for neglecting to respond promptly to an emergency call.

When a competition is an organised event, the organiser must obtain police approval before staging it. Regulations mandate that the police must have officers on standby, likely accompanied by a police van, to ensure the event runs safely and smoothly.

People with disabilities are no longer confined to their homes. There are numerous ways in which the government and charitable organisations provide support to enhance their mobility. One significant initiative is the provision of wheelchairs. These are supplied by the government based on the recommendation of a medical doctor after a thorough series of tests and examinations. Modern wheelchairs are designed not just for transportation but also for convenience. They feature storage spaces, either at the back or beneath the seat, enabling users to carry groceries when shopping or store snacks and drinks for outings to public parks, exercise locations, or sightseeing trips.

Additionally, these wheelchairs are now electrically powered, with removable batteries that can be charged when not in use. The welfare policy of the United Kingdom aims to maximise independence and mobility for everyone, leveraging technology to achieve this goal. Ongoing research, backed by universities, laboratories, and NGOs, ensures that the welfare of disabled individuals continuously evolves, reflecting the belief that every person deserves the right to live a full and fulfilling life.

However, for these facilities and advancements to function effectively, roads and pavements must be well-maintained and meet the required standards. In Nigeria, the rapid expansion of towns is not matched by proportional road development. Many urban roads are riddled with potholes, poorly tarred, and lack proper drainage. After rainfalls, roads become flooded, and vehicles often splash water onto pedestrians on pavements. Such incidents force people to return home to change into clean attire, causing unnecessary inconvenience.

Children, particularly school children, often suffer from malnourishment and a lack of basic necessities, including shoes. In such conditions, it is unrealistic to expect these children to use tricycles or skateboards on muddy roads, which can even cause adults to slip and fall. Drivers, meanwhile, often honk their vehicle horns in an aggressive, demeaning manner, shouting abusive language at pedestrians–disregarding marked pedestrian crossings and failing to consider the health or limitations of elderly people walking slowly across the road. It is vital to remember that not all disabilities are immediately visible.

We must respect children, women, and people with disabilities.

CHAPTER TWENTY-THREE

THE CONCEPT OF AFRICAN TIMES

It was amusing in those years to observe how my methods of getting things done appeared to others. My insistence on tasks being completed within a specific timeframe and to a particular standard seemed almost absurd to those involved. When a task relied on someone else's input, they resented my urging them to act promptly, especially at designated times. Everyone perceived my concern as bossy, dictatorial, or as evidence that I lacked an understanding of workplace ethics or the challenges others faced. Yet, those same individuals would gather in groups, laughing and joking about matters unrelated to their assigned duties.

However, one fact remained inescapable: when deadlines were missed or objectives unaccomplished, the consequences fell solely on me. I would bear the brunt of blame, disciplinary actions, or even dismissal. This would give them satisfaction, allowing them to spread gossip: 'Have you heard? So-and-so has been sacked!' - conveniently forgetting that their inaction contributed directly to my predicament.

I have always valued punctuality and preparation. Whenever I was invited to an event–academic conferences, social gatherings, or medical appointments–it became second nature to arrive 15 minutes before the scheduled time. This habit allowed me to engage with like-minded individuals, fostering connections before proceedings began. Over time, punctuality became an intrinsic part of my identity. Yet, others would ridicule me, jokingly asking why I consistently arrived early: 'Are you there to help arrange the hall?'

One memorable incident occurred at a naming ceremony held at an event centre in Dalston, Hackney. The invitation stated the party would begin at 8 p.m. and end by midnight. As was my custom, I left my home in Manor Park at 6 p.m., mindful of the multiple transfers required–travelling by underground on different lines, then switching to a bus. I arrived at the hall at 7:50 p.m., only to find the doors locked and the venue unprepared. By 9:30 p.m., feeling chilled by the weather, I decided to head home.

On my way, I encountered a relative of the celebrant, who persuaded me to return and keep him company. He called the hosts, only to discover they were just waking up and had yet to begin dressing for the event! Reluctantly, I waited with him as the party's start was delayed until 10:30 p.m. Eventually, it transformed into an all-night affair.

Over the years, I have noticed a peculiar phenomenon at social events: some attendees arrive only when the gathering is winding down. When asked, they nonchalantly claim they 'like to take their time.'

In Nigeria in earlier days, parties were often celebrated on the streets, blocking neighbourhoods and hindering motorists' access. Events might also spill over into neighbours' expansive yards. However, this practice later required official permission from the local town council, usually sought two weeks in advance. A small fee was mandated to approve street closures. Nowadays, such celebrations are prohibited entirely, and parties are typically held in hired halls or event centres. While costly, this shift signifies progress, reflecting a growing sense of modernity and civility.

The concept of *African time* encapsulates our culture's approach to time–where we allow it to dictate our actions rather than the reverse, as seen in more developed nations. For instance, in the United Kingdom, some schools and churches rent out their halls for public events to generate income. Interestingly, some churches even set aside theological objections to alcohol to facilitate celebrations. This recalls the Biblical narrative of Jesus turning water into wine at a wedding in Galilee, ensuring the guests' enjoyment and sparing the groom from embarrassment. Ultimately, we are all human, and accommodating each other's needs during significant moments should always be a priority.

In the UK, when you are permitted to use a hall, even though you are required to pay a levy for its use, you will be given a specific start time for your event and a mandatory end time. Every hall, whether attached to schools, churches, or council-owned facilities, employs staff responsible for maintaining order within the venue and its surroundings. This is often necessary due to complaints from neighbouring residents about disturbances, which are frequently reported to law enforcement agencies, particularly the police.

Once the allocated time is up, no amount of pleading will extend it. I have attended some Nigerian events where hall staff were forced to disconnect electric plugs from the sockets, plunging the venue into complete darkness. The celebrants and guests had to use mobile phone torches to navigate their way out, while musicians or DJs hurriedly removed their equipment.

On such occasions, it is common to hear Nigerians berating the staff for simply doing their lawful duties. However, what has a beginning must have an end–this is a condition already agreed upon when paying for the hall's use. It is impossible to influence hall staff as they are often constrained by complaints from neighbouring residents, whose parking spaces may have been occupied by guests' numerous vehicles. Furthermore, if the event is a Nigerian party, it is not uncommon to see a police car stationed outside as a precautionary measure.

In the 21st century, nobody has the freedom to act entirely as they please, whenever they please. Laws and regulations exist, and compliance with them is essential for maintaining order. To be progressive, modern, and aligned with developed nations, we must adhere to structured time management. Africa does not operate on an exclusive timeframe and must strive to be proactive, rather than reactive, in all aspects of our dealings.

CHAPTER TWENTY-FOUR

LIFE COULD BE MADE BETTER

Every human being is susceptible to minor or major illnesses at some point in life, which may arise unexpectedly under any circumstances. For governments to ensure their citizens contribute meaningfully to society, adequate arrangements must be in place to guarantee that healthcare facilities and equipment are available in hospitals, thereby making public health a top priority.

Illnesses have been detected in children even before birth, often identified through clinical tests, examinations, or ultrasound scans. Unfortunately, many African hospitals lack the willingness to procure and install such essential equipment. While some clinical departments possess the requisite manpower, their expertise can be further enhanced by inviting foreign professionals to train local staff or by sponsoring medical personnel to attend training programmes, courses, or conferences abroad.

Regrettably, governments of African nations often cite inadequate funding as the reason for failing to invest in crucial healthcare infrastructure. Yet, we witness politicians in legislative chambers purchasing luxury vehicles valued at 156 million Naira each. National newspapers frequently report that members of these chambers earn as much as ₦28 million per month, excluding numerous allowances. By comparison, one can only speculate on the staggering sums earned and expended by state governors and their families monthly.

Allow me to narrate an incident reported several years ago regarding the Lagos State General Hospital in Surulere to you. The World Health Organization donated medical equipment to the hospital for clinical testing and patient examinations. Shockingly, these items were abandoned outside the hospital for over five years without being installed. Ultimately, the equipment deteriorated became unusable, and was either discarded or stolen. This unfortunate episode epitomises the neglect pervasive in Nigerian institutions, where public welfare is often disregarded.

The causes of illness are numerous and, in many cases, preventable. Examples include open defecation due to a lack of public toilets, improper waste management, and overcrowding, all of which can lead to the spread of contagious diseases. State and local governments bear the responsibility of addressing such issues to prevent outbreaks and safeguard public health.

Hospitals must be government-owned, adequately staffed, and effectively managed to ensure the control of diseases and the promotion of public welfare. Citizens should feel confident seeking medical attention for any health concerns, however minor, aligning with the adage that 'prevention is better than cure.' Sadly, many resort to self-medication or consulting unqualified chemists because hospital fees are exorbitantly high, making proper healthcare inaccessible to the average citizen.

Consider the case of a 13-year-old girl named Jomiloju Poroye[4]. Born prematurely, her condition might have been prevented had her mother undergone thorough prenatal testing and ultrasound examinations. The financial burden of Jomiloju's medical treatments fell entirely on her mother, as her father abandoned them both. Despite paying millions of Naira for surgeries, including one to connect the child's ears to her brain, the mother exhausted her resources. The hospital currently demands N14.6 million for further treatments, stalling the child's recovery. Over three years, Jomiloju's mother tirelessly moved from one hospital to another, seeking surgeries and tests that yielded no definitive resolution. Remarkably, Jomiloju survived and has become a celebrated painter, a testament to her resilience and her mother's dedication. However, this story underscores the government's failure to provide adequate support for its citizens.

The persistent lack of investment in healthcare infrastructure and services by African governments is a dire situation. Addressing these shortcomings is not only a moral obligation but also essential for fostering a healthier and more productive society. The plight of individuals like Jomiloju highlights the urgent need for systemic reforms in healthcare policies, funding, and execution.

Contrary to the aforementioned situation, in the UK, the doctor responsible for delivering a baby would have written a medical report on the child's condition to the NHS, enabling a referral to a specialist hospital equipped to treat similar cases. The treatment of the child would then become the responsibility

---

[4] The case was reported by Ola Awakan on his YouTube Channel.

of the government health system from birth. This process reflects the system in the United Kingdom, where the NHS ensures that the needs of citizens, regardless of their age or the cause of their illness, are not left to parents to manage, as seems to be the case here.

In the UK, once a resident reaches the age of 60, local government entities assume partial responsibility for their health, finances, and welfare. A notable feature of this system is the Accident and Emergency (A&E) service, which operates 24/7. Any individual can walk into a hospital, register at reception, describe their health concerns, and wait to be seen on a first-come, first-served basis. There is no prioritisation based on social connections or status. If the issue requires only medication, it is provided promptly, and the patient is discharged. Should admission be necessary, a hospital bed is made available, or the patient is transferred to a facility specialising in the required treatment, often by ambulance.

Once a citizen turns 60, they are entitled to free GP consultations for crucial but routine areas such as blood tests, eye exams, and dental care. Prescription medication is also provided at no cost from nearby pharmacies or chemists, based on prescriptions from GPs. Additionally, the NHS frequently promotes free vaccinations for flu, COVID-19, and other diseases for individuals aged 75 and above. Numerous clinics provide these services, and making an appointment is as simple as a phone call, after which reminders are sent via mobile text messages.

In cases of emergencies, accidents are inevitable, but help is prompt. Anyone can call emergency services, and a police car or ambulance typically arrives within 10 to 15 minutes. A failure to respond within this timeframe can lead to legal action against the NHS, resulting in penalties or fines for negligence.

For residents aged 60 and over, special travel provisions, such as the Freedom Pass, facilitate movement within London. This card, issued every two years and renewable upon request, allows free travel on the London Underground, Overground trains, and surface trains within the city. It applies during off-peak hours from 9 a.m. until the end of service.

The government also provides rebates on essential items for elderly residents, complementing their state pensions. Council accommodation residents, for instance, may qualify for rent and water bill discounts, with water corporations obligated to reduce charges for eligible households.

Until the Labour Party's election victory in 2024, elderly citizens above a certain age received a Winter Fuel Allowance to help with heating costs during the winter months. However, the Labour government's 2034 budget eliminated this allowance, despite its absence from their campaign manifesto. This decision may lead to increased cases of pneumonia and premature deaths among vulnerable populations.

Blessed with abundant crude oil resources, Nigeria ought to have leaders who prioritise using this revenue for the welfare of its citizens. Instead, headlines are rife with reports of public officials engaging in gross misconduct. For instance, allegations of the Accountant General embezzling ₦109 billion and state governors misappropriating security votes have become commonplace. Retired military personnel have resorted to protesting at the Federal Ministry of Finance, shutting it down to compel pension payments. How many pensioners remain unpaid today?

One of the leading national newspapers in Nigeria shockingly published that the EFCC found $800 million and ₦750 million in El-Rufai the former governor of Kaduna State's son, but the EFCC has refuted the report as fake news. If these allegations were true, one must ask: how did someone of his age and experience amass such vast sums?

Furthermore, the lack of infrastructure in Nigeria's hospitals has prompted a mass exodus of trained medical professionals–including doctors, nurses, and specialists–seeking better opportunities abroad. These developed nations now reap the benefits of expertise Nigeria cultivated at great expense. It is perplexing how many of Nigeria's leaders, having been educated or trained in countries such as the UK and USA, fail to implement the systems and principles they once observed and enjoyed. This dissonance remains a tragic mystery.

ABOUT THE AUTHOR

OLATUNJI OLUSANYA is an octogenarian whose passion for writing explores life's complexities and the pressing issues within society. A fervent advocate for justice, human dignity, and societal reform, he draws on decades of experience to offer a deeply personal and insightful perspective on governance, human rights, and social equity.

Born in Ago-Iwoye, Ogun State, Nigeria, Olatunji is deeply rooted in family values and cultural heritage while embracing the importance of adapting to change. His writings aim to illuminate vital social issues, provoke reflection, and inspire action for a fairer and more just society.

Olatunji Olusanya currently resides in the United Kingdom, where he is actively involved in social commentary, community advocacy, and mentorship. He deploys his wisdom and life lessons to empower future generations.

www.ingramcontent.com/pod-product-compliance
Lightning Source LLC
LaVergne TN
LVHW020441070526
838199LV00063B/4805